# The Somerville Arts Council presents
# Nibble

## Exploring food, art and culture in Union Square—and beyond

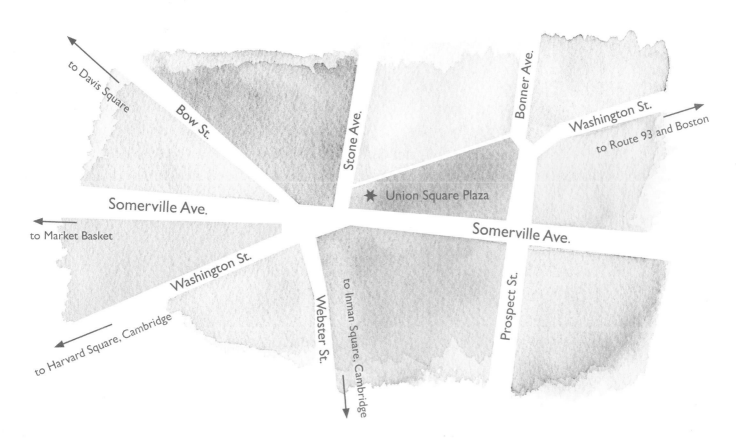

to Davis Square

Bow St.

Stone Ave.

Bonner Ave.

Washington St.

to Route 93 and Boston

Union Square Plaza

Somerville Ave.

to Market Basket

Somerville Ave.

Washington St.

Prospect St.

to Harvard Square, Cambridge

Webster St.

to Inman Square, Cambridge

A Somerville Arts Council Publication
Copyright 2012; first printing July, 2012
Without limiting the rights under copyright reserved above, no part of this publication may be reproduced, stored in or introduced into a retrieval system, or transmitted, in any form, or by any means (electronic, mechanical, photocopying, recording, or otherwise) without prior written permission of both the copyright owner and the publisher of this book.

ISBN 978-0-615-65464-5

Somerville Arts Council
50 Evergreen Avenue
Somerville, MA 02145

# THANKS

ArtsUnion is funded by the Massachusetts Cultural Council's Adams Arts Program and the City of Somerville.

They say too many cooks spoil the broth, but when it comes to this book, the opposite is true! Over the course of a year, more than 50 people worked towards making *Nibble* a reality. The vast majority of writers, photographers, artists, cooks and recipe testers contributed their time and talents on a voluntary basis—and we are so grateful.

Cooks like Ana Flores and Judith Laguerre invited us into their homes to share their culinary talents. Photographers like Dustin Kerstein hauled gear all over town to shoot dish after dish. Recipe testers like Katherine Perry and Catherine Aiello offered practical cooking wisdom. Thanks also to Joan Handwerg, Ilan Mochari, Beth Forrest, Robert Smyth, Deborah Pacini and especially Susan Abbattista for sage editorial ideas and guidance.

It has been a pleasure working with Union Square's food businesses; thanks for your patience with our questions—we hope you like this book! We also appreciate the help of Mimi Graney, who never tires of our queries, and Ngaio Schiff, who helps coordinate the Intercambio Language and Culture Exchange. Meri Jenkins at the Massachusetts Cultural Council has been a champion of our ArtsUnion work from the start; Meri, we always appreciate your encouragement and input.

Years ago, a fabulous volunteer named Sharon Wolfson launched our Union Square International Market Tours. Sharon, this book started with you! More recently, we have had some great interns, including Elysian McNiff, Sarah Champion and Raleigh Strott, who all contributed to this book. Most of all, we thank our marvelous multilingual Arts Council intern and managing editor Vera Vidal, who played a crucial role in helping us complete this project. *Vera, nous t'adorons!* —The Somerville Arts Council

| | |
|---|---|
| Editor & Creative Director | Rachel Strutt |
| Managing Editor | Vera Vidal |
| Graphic Designer | Meagan O'Brien |
| | www.meaganobrien.com |
| Copy Editor | David Plunkett |
| Nibble Editorial Interns | Sarah Champion, Elysian McNiff, Raleigh Strott |
| Primary Photographers | Rachel Blumenthal |
| | www.rachelblumenthal.net |
| | Caleb Cole |
| | www.calebcolephoto.com |
| | Dustin Kerstein |
| | www.dustinkerstein.com |

Additional photographers: Nathan Boucher, Amy Braga, Stan Czesniuk, Geoff Hargadon, Somerby Jones, Alexis Kochka, Elysian McNiff, Bess Paupeck, Olivia Peters, Clarissa Sosin, Rachel Strutt, Alex Zucker

Artists: Catherine Aiello, Heather Balchunas, Francisco de la Barra, Sarah Coyne (www.eggagogo.com), Judith Klausner, Meagan O'Brien

Writers: Susan Abbattista, Valeria Amato, Shannon Cain Arnold, Heather Balchunas, Julie Betters, Brother Cleve, Aaron Cohen, June Carolyn Erlick, Julia Fairclough, Beth Forrest, Mary Goodman, Kathleen Hennessey, Gregory Jenkins, Alexis Kochka, Jarrett Lerner, Susan Llewelyn Leach, Leah Gourley Lindsay, Elysian McNiff, Deirdre Murphy, Genevieve Rajewski, Jill Sahil, Rebecca Small, Raleigh Strott, Rachel Strutt, Vera Vidal, Anna Larson Williams, Sharon Wolfson

Recipe authors: Lucia Austria, Julie Betters, Brother Cleve, Alberto Cabré, Cory Clarke, Maria Curtatone, Elizabete Delfino, Jill Downer, Ana Flores, Mary Goodman, William Gilson, the Journeyman Chefs, Alexis Kochka, Judith Laguerre, Leah Gourley Lindsay, Mark Romano, Shanker Sahil, Rachel Strutt, Bimala Thapa, Rongwen Zhang

Recipe testers: Catherine Aiello, Heather Balchunas, Julie Betters, Rachel Blumenthal, Alex Buchanan, Julia Fairclough, Beth Forrest, Ellen Kramer, Anna Larson, Leah Gourley Lindsay, Christine McLellan, Flinn Metternick, Deirdre Murphy, Meagan O'Brien, Bess Paupeck, Katherine Perry, Ryan Redmond, Rachel Strutt, Lisa Young

# LETTER FROM THE MAYOR

The mayor with his mother, Maria. For Maria's tiella di Gaeta recipe, go to page 65.

Growing up I learned a lot about cooking from my mother. She emigrated from Gaeta, Italy, to Somerville with my father in the 1950s. I used to watch her make endless sauces and tiella di Gaeta—a savory tart made with a variety of fillings. Yet I didn't just watch; my mom let me roll up my sleeves and chop vegetables, knead dough and stir sauces. I like to think I learned from the best. To this day, I love cooking.

I grew up just outside Union Square, where I lived until a few years ago. Over the years I have seen it transform in many ways. It has been particularly exciting to see the square become a recognized food destination and entertainment hub. With new restaurants opening at a fast clip—places like Ebi Sushi, Casa B, Fortissimo Café—and an ever-expanding selection of diverse markets and restaurants, there's no denying that Union Square is gaining popularity around the region. You will get a taste of this simply by reading this book!

One of my favorite things about Somerville is the tremendous variety of food from around the globe that can be found within our borders. We are a city rich in history, culture, diversity and food, and all of this makes us one of the most up-and-coming destinations in the nation. Although this book focuses on Union Square, you can find samples of our diverse culinary landscape throughout the city. Teele Square offers Indian, Turkish and Nepali cuisine all on one block. In Davis, there's Mexican, Italian and fabulous BBQ. In East Somerville, amidst Brazilian, Ethiopian and Salvadoran eating options, new restaurants like East End Grill are joining the culinary community. What's happening in Union reflects a citywide trend. Through ArtsUnion funding, we're offering you a glimpse of this trend, our city—and the world—through one of our vibrant squares.

We are proud of our diverse neighborhoods and the local flavor our numerous independently owned businesses bring to Somerville. I look forward to seeing you at one of the restaurants featured in this book!

Happy eating,

*Joseph A. Curtatone*

Joseph A. Curtatone, Mayor

# OUR INSATIABLE APPETITE

**The Somerville Arts Council explains its obsession with food and Union Square.**

The Flufferettes perform at Union Square Main Streets' annual What the Fluff? festival.

A fire performer at the Arts Council's Hungry Tiger Street Food Festival.

Henry Patterson pours Thai sangrias for folks on a recent Somerville Arts Council tasting tour.

Eating your way through Union Square—Portuguese porridge for breakfast, a giant masala dosa for lunch, pad kra-pow for dinner, followed by some local brews at a pub—is like taking a vicarious spin around the globe, while remaining fiercely local. The square's collective menu offers food from afar, like Amazonian açaí and Korean kimchi, as well as locally made items like Capone Foods' squid ink pasta and Fiore de Nonno's honey lavender and chili burrata. We find this mix of international and local fare quite tasty indeed.

You may wonder, why does an Arts Council have such an insatiable appetite for food? To answer that question, let's rewind to 2005, when we received an Adams Arts Program Grant from the Massachusetts Cultural Council to spur the cultural economy of Union Square. With this grant, our ArtsUnion project was born. And it has been thriving ever since, with outdoor festivals and markets, new street furniture and banners in the square, new arts-friendly zoning—and a heaping portion of food-related programming.

From the start of ArtsUnion, we have aimed to cultivate and celebrate the existing cultural assets of Union Square: food, diversity and a vibrant arts community. Among other initiatives, we launched walking tours of the square's international markets—taking visitors to Casa de Carne, La Internacional and New Bombay, to name just a few. Over the years, we've led restaurant tasting tours and produced foodie events like Project Yum, which included an Iron Chef competition; the Hungry Tiger Street Food Festival; and, of course, the What the Fluff? festival, curated by our ArtsUnion partner, Union Square Main Streets.

We have found that food not only propels cultural tourism, it is a universal form of expression that conveys countless stories about cultural identity. For example, over the years, we've noticed that local markets stock their shelves in relation to the cultural calendars of local immigrant communities: WellFoods Plus sells endless boxes of Medjool dates for Ramadan, and La Internacional sells heaps of bacalao around Easter. We've also noticed how food piques the interest of local artists, who use it as a subject and a medium. Who says you can't paint with turmeric or create cameos using Oreo cookies?

To share some of the food stories we've gathered, we launched Nibble, a blog about the intersection of food, art and culture in Union Square. The blog then spawned this book. In these pages, we explore how food tells a story about the Union Square community *and* plays an important place-making role. We think the square is a very special neighborhood right now; it is diverse, artsy, yet has enough grit to keep things interesting. This is illustrated through the food landscape, with its beautiful, motley mix of pizza joints, mom-and-pop markets, lively pubs, bustling farmers' markets, posh new restaurants and brimming global flavor. This book aims to capture this dynamic—and delicious—sense of place.

Beyond articles and interviews with artists, restaurateurs and shopkeepers, Nibble offers you recipes aplenty. Because there's a story behind every dish, we include recipe introductions—allowing you to meet the cooks and discover the curious and circuitous history of Fluff, for example.

So, yes, we're obsessed with food these days. But we're not alone. The city's Shape Up Somerville program, Union Square Main Streets, East Somerville Main Streets and the Welcome Project are other local organizations promoting food as a way to celebrate healthy living, promote diversity and spur the local economy. Collectively, we're putting Somerville on the gastronomic map. —*The Somerville Arts Council*

A Somerville Iron Chef contest at the Arts Council's Project Yum festival in 2007.

Rachel Strutt (far left) of the Somerville Arts Council leads a Union Square Market Tour.

**About the recipes:** You will find a range, from simple to complex, local-leaning to exotic. A small army of Nibble cooks have tested all of these dishes. Recipes have been tweaked accordingly to ensure that cooks of all levels can recreate these dishes at home. Rather than include recipes from each Union Square restaurant, we encourage you to hit the square and explore its many eateries!

# The Nibble Menu

 ARTICLE    RECIPE    RESTAURANTS    MARKETS AND FOOD PRODUCERS

## Breakfast

10 | THIS BUDDY'S FOR YOU: PORTRAIT OF A DINER

12 | DONUT MUFFINS

14 | LEMON RICOTTA PANCAKES WITH BLUEBERRY SAUCE

16 | SCRAMBLED EGGS WITH FLOR DE IZOTE, LOROCO PUPUSAS

## Appetizers

MARKET BASKET: THE MULTIETHNIC MAGNET | 20

A FRUITFUL EXCHANGE: PORTRAITS AND GLOBAL FOOD STORIES | 25

CURED BLUEFISH AND GOUGÈRES | 32

SRI LANKAN HOPPERS WITH MISO-GLAZED BARBECUED EGGPLANT | 35

SOPA AZTECA | 38

GINGER CHICKEN WINGS | 40

## Entrees

44 | LATIN FLAVOR: THE SQUARE'S LATINO RESTAURATEURS

53 | PAINTING WITH PAPRIKA: AN INTERVIEW WITH FRANCISCO DE LA BARRA

56 | NEPALI KIDNEY BEAN CURRY, PULAO & TOMATO TIMUR PICKLE

60 | OKRA ETOUFFÉE, RIZ AU DJON DJON & FRIED PLANTAINS

64 | TIELLA DI GAETA

67 | SPICY COCONUT CURRIED GOAT STEW

# Locavore & Healthy Fare

HOME GROWN: THE SQUARE'S LOCAVORE MOVEMENT  | 72

SPRING GARDEN SALAD & WONTONS WITH CHILI DIPPING SAUCE | 77

FARMER CHEESE & RED PEPPER SALAD WITH TOASTED PINENUTS | 80

NORTH INDIAN DAL & ROTI | 83

# Desserts

88 | COOKIE CAMEOS: AN INTERVIEW WITH JUDITH KLAUSNER

91 | FLUFF S'MORES BRÛLÉE

94 | MERENGÓN DE FRESA

98 | TAZA CHOCOLATE BEIGNETS WITH COFFEE CRÈME ANGLAISE

102 | BRAZILIAN BRIGADEIRO

# Wine, Cocktails & Nibbles

URBAN VINEYARDS: A PROFILE OF TWO WINEMAKERS | 106

WORLD PARTY: GLOBAL COCKTAILS & NIBBLES | 109

THE UNION & POLENTA ROUNDS WITH ROASTED TOMATO JAM AND CHORIZO | 110

CURRIED SCALLOP CAKES WITH CILANTRO PESTO & THE MAHARAJA'S REVENGE | 112

PERU NEGRO & "CEVICHE" WITH AJÍ AMARILLLO | 114

PORK MEATBALLS WITH SOY-WASABI SAUCE & SEOUL KISS | 116

# Union Square Guide

118 | MARKETS AND FOOD PRODUCERS

123 | RESTAURANTS

Clockwise from top left: the breakfast rush at Bloc 11; the espresso machine at Fortissimo, one of Union Square's new cafes; a blender "cosy" in the kitchen of Ana Flores; the breakfast crowd at the Neighborhood; Ana Flores demonstrates how to make scrambled eggs with flor de izote; lemon ricotta pancakes—perhaps the best stack of pancakes we've ever tasted.

Clarissa Sosin

Rachel Strutt

## Breakfast

 THIS BUDDY'S FOR YOU

 DONUT MUFFINS

 LEMON RICOTTA PANCAKES WITH BLUEBERRY SAUCE

 SCRAMBLED EGGS WITH FLOR DE IZOTE, LOROCO PUPUSAS

# THIS BUDDY'S FOR YOU

**Illustrator Heather Balchunas paints a vivid portrait of Buddy's Truck Stop, just outside Union Square.**

Text & Illustrations: Heather Balchunas

As a longtime fan of roadside Americana, I like to eat in diners *and* illustrate them. Like many, I can't resist their retro-chic charm and crowd-pleasing comfort food. Diners also have a certain mystique about them, as if they have stories to tell. In the case of Buddy's Truck Stop, located on Washington Street between Union Square and Sullivan Square, there certainly *is* a story—many in fact.

Buddy's is a shining example of the diners produced by the Worcester Lunch Car Company in the 1920s and 1930s. The stainless steel boxcar exterior is modest and unassuming. Inside, Buddy's boasts black-and-white checkered tiles, swivel stools and a rose marble countertop; this intimate 20-seater radiates signature early diner style. In the early-morning hours, with the soft green neon glow from the overhead lights, and just a few customers inside, you'll feel like you've stepped into an Edward Hopper painting.

Before coming to Somerville in 1951, this 1930 Worcester diner was "parked" in Leominster, where it was known as Sawin's Diner. Shortly after the boxcar was hauled into the 'ville, Buddy Barrett—the diner's namesake—bought the place and opened up shop. Years later, he turned it over to his 21-year-old son, John Barrett, who ran the place with his wife, Sue, for four decades. In 2005, the Barretts decided to sell. Then something interesting happened: Nicole Bairos, just 22 at the time, saw the FOR SALE sign in Buddy's window, marched in and asked the Barretts to hold the diner for her with a down payment, which they did. Six months later, with the financing squared away, Bairos became the owner of this classic diner. Her laid-back, lively banter fits right in with the atmosphere at Buddy's—a crossroads of cultures where hipsters, truckers and locals can converge over a cup o' joe, swap stories and watch the game.

Daily specials at Buddy's are handwritten on paper plates hung along the back wall. Just like this "menu," the fare is simple and no-nonsense; it is also generously portioned and sinfully satisfying. You won't leave hungry—especially if you manage to finish the tasty hash. ●

# DONUT MUFFINS

**We have been intrigued by these curious hybrid confections ever since their debut at Sherman Cafe.**

Cory Clarke, baker at Sherman Cafe, had been looking for a good doughnut recipe when, one day while watching *The Best Thing I Ever Ate* on the Food Network, a woman raved about a doughnut muffin she had eaten. Perfect, thought Cory. Here was a way to bake a doughnut and eschew frying, something that would be difficult in Sherman's kitchen. Cory then developed a recipe while retaining the key ingredient to any worthy doughnut: nutmeg!

Above: the decadent finished product; right: Sherman Cafe baker Cory Clarke demonstrates how to coat the muffins with sugar.

Recipe: **Cory Clarke** | Photography: **Rachel Blumenthal** | Recipe Testing: **Katherine Perry**

# DONUT MUFFINS   Makes 12 small muffins

**Recipe tip**: If you'd like, you can skip the last three steps—although we think the cinnamon coating makes these muffins even more delicious!

## Ingredients

½ pound butter, at room temperature
2 eggs, at room temperature
1 cup sugar (plus 1 cup for topping)
½ teaspoon baking soda
1 tablespoon baking powder

½ teaspoon salt
3 cups flour
1 cup plain yogurt
2 teaspoons nutmeg
2 tablespoons cinnamon

## Directions

1. Cream ½ pound butter with an electric mixer (use paddle attachment if you have one). Add 1 cup of sugar, and whip on medium-high speed until fluffy (about 3 minutes).
2. Add baking soda, baking powder, and salt and mix well, stopping the mixer to scrape the bottom and sides of the bowl, making sure everything is fully incorporated.
3. Add eggs and beat on medium-high until batter is fluffy and resembles custard.
4. Add 1½ cups flour and mix well (again scrape sides and bottom of bowl).
5. Add ½ cup yogurt and mix well.
6. Add nutmeg and mix well.
7. Add 1½ cups flour and mix in spurts, taking care not to overwork the batter.
8. Add ½ cup yogurt and mix, again taking care not to overwork the batter.
9. Prepare 12 small muffin tins with canola oil spray.

10. Put batter into muffin tins so that each tin is slightly mounded with dough.
11. Bake at 350°F for approximately 25-30 minutes, rotating tins halfway through the baking time. Muffins should be golden brown, and a toothpick inserted in the center should come out with a few moist crumbs. Allow the muffins to cool for about 15 minutes.
12. Melt some additional butter in the microwave or on the stove top and prepare a small bowl with 1 cup sugar and 2 tablespoons cinnamon mixed together
13. Roll each muffin top in the melted butter and place upright on a paper towel to allow the butter to soak into each muffin.
14. Roll each muffin top in the cinnamon sugar mixture and serve.

# LEMON-RICOTTA PANCAKES WITH BLUEBERRY SAUCE

**After taking a ricotta-making class at Capone Foods, a baking enthusiast perfects a recipe for a stunning stack of pancakes—using ricotta as the star ingredient.**

Leah Gourley Lindsay, who lives just outside Union Square, made countless batches of lemon-ricotta pancakes to come up with this final recipe. After a bite of these pancakes, we think you will concur: her efforts paid off!

I have fond childhood memories of feasting on ricotta gnocchi made by my great-grandmother Angelina. She lived near Pittsburgh, but her parents emigrated from Southern Italy, so her gnocchi was the real deal. So I was pleased to discover a ricotta-making class offered at Capone Foods, a small shop in Union Square packed with a broad range of Italian staples and prepared frozen meals, like strata, various lasagnas and fregola with mushrooms.

During the class, shop proprietor Al Capone demonstrated how simple it is to coax just a few ingredients—milk, cream, vinegar, salt—into a sumptuous batch of ricotta. The final product was a revelation, and I have been making my own ever since. You may be wondering: Is it worth the effort? Yes! Homemade ricotta boasts a rich, velvety texture that eclipses the bland, mass-produced version found in stores.

Ricotta is amazingly versatile, in Italian cuisine and beyond. In our four-hour class, Capone showed us how to use ricotta to make gnocchi, tortelloni and a baked ricotta dessert. In other classes, apparently, he has taught students how to make ricotta-Nutella empanadas! Left to my own devices, I have used batches of ricotta to make my great-grandma's gnocchi, orange-scented pound cake—and these pancakes.

Ricotta transforms a lackluster stack of pancakes into a bright, airy affair. And using both lemon juice and zest subtly boosts the tangy flavor. Pancakes may be an American favorite, but the ricotta in this recipe nods to my Italian heritage, so I say: *Buon appetito!*

Recipe and Text: Leah Gourley Lindsay | Photography: Dustin Kerstein | Recipe Testing: Katherine Perry

# LEMON RICOTTA PANCAKES  Serves 4-5

## Ingredients

1¼ cups all-purpose flour
3 tablespoons granulated sugar
2 teaspoons baking powder
½ teaspoon baking soda
¼ teaspoon salt
1 cup ricotta cheese*

1 large egg
2 large egg whites
½ cup fresh lemon juice
2 teaspoons grated lemon zest
¼ cup milk
Optional: fresh blueberries

## Directions

1. In a large bowl, whisk together dry ingredients.
2. In a medium bowl, stir together ricotta cheese, egg, egg whites, lemon juice, lemon zest, and milk. Gently fold this mixture into the dry ingredients until flour is incorporated. Don't overmix; the batter will be thicker than traditional pancake batter.
3. Heat a griddle or a nonstick skillet over medium heat. Spray with cooking spray or brush butter on the cooking surface. Drop about ⅓ cup of batter onto the hot griddle or skillet. You can spread the batter out with the back of a spoon or use a circular mold to form round pancakes. Optional: Add a few blueberries to the pancakes once they are on the skillet or griddle.
4. Cook the pancakes until browned on the underside and beginning to set, about 5 minutes. Flip and cook on the other side, about 3 minutes longer. Serve warm with blueberry sauce.

*Shopping tip: Buy freshly made ricotta at Capone's. Or consider making your own; check www.caponefoods.com for cooking classes.

# BLUEBERRY SAUCE

## Ingredients

1½ tablespoons fresh lemon juice
1½ teaspoons cornstarch
2 cups fresh or frozen blueberries
2 tablespoons granulated sugar
2 tablespoons water

## Directions

1. In a small bowl, combine the lemon juice and cornstarch and set aside.
2. In a medium saucepan, combine the blueberries, sugar, and water. Bring to a boil over medium-high heat, stirring occasionally.
3. Reduce to a simmer; stir in lemon juice and cornstarch mixture (give it a little stir to recombine if necessary). Stir until the sauce thickens slightly. Cover to keep warm, and set aside.

# SCRAMBLED EGGS WITH FLOR DE IZOTE, LOROCO PUPUSAS

**Ana Flores reminisces about the flavors and flowers of her native El Salvador.**

Ana Flores with her daughter, Klara Salamanca.

A plastic flor de izote plant at La Internacional.

When Ana Flores was growing up in El Salvador, she would walk to her grandparents' house each day to pick flowers from their garden for cooking. The flor de izote, also known as yucca, is Salvador's national flower and a breakfast delicacy. The plant's flowers are clustered in a pyramid of blooms far beyond the reach of children's hands. So with the help of her grandfather, Ana would chop a stalk down and run home to watch her mother cook the blossoms with eggs.

Now living in Somerville with children of her own, Ana only whips up a traditional breakfast on special occasions. In addition to eggs with flor de izote, a morning meal with the Flores family also might include pupusas with loroco, another flower used in Salvadoran cuisine.

Cooking with fresh blossoms was only part of the magic of Ana's childhood in Yucuaiquin, in the east of El Salvador. They had no electricity or running water, but a diet of fresh foods that would be the envy of any urban foodie. "At our house, my father kept bees; the honey was delicious," Ana recalls. "Around my grandparents' house, there were mangoes, lemon and lime trees, jocote, annonas and flor de izote. Organic food isn't new to me; it's what I grew up with."

"We didn't have a stove, so we cooked over a fire," she continues. "We cooked in clay pots, which gave the food a certain taste—I really liked the taste. Now they have stoves back home. We are helping modernize the country by sending some money back home."

Recipes: Ana Flores | Text: Susan Llewelyn Leach | Photography: Rachel Strutt (this page) & Clarissa Sosin (right)
Recipe Testing: Catherine Aiello

**Recipe tip:** Ana serves pupusas with curtido salad and a tomato salsa; find these recipes at the recipe section at www.somervilleartscouncil.org/nibble.

**\*Shopping tip:** Find these ingredients at La Internacional and other Latino markets.

## LOROCO PUPUSAS   Makes 10-12 pupusas

### Ingredients
1¼ pounds shredded white cheddar
1 6-ounce packet of frozen flor de loroco*
1 pound masa de maiz (Ana uses Maseca brand)*
3½ cups water
1½ tablespoons olive oil

### Directions
1. Finely chop loroco and combine with shredded cheddar in a large bowl. Knead by hand for 5 minutes until the mixture sticks together.
2. In a separate bowl pour in the masa flour and slowly add 3½ cups of water, kneading as you go until the dough is smooth (about 10 minutes). If the dough seems dry when kneading, add a little more water.
3. To make the individual pupusas, take a small fist-size ball of masa dough and flatten it into a shallow bowl in the palm of your hand.
4. With the other hand take a smaller ball of loroco mix, place it at the center of the dough bowl and gently flatten it out to the edges of the bowl. Moisten palms with olive oil and shape the dough into a ball around the loroco, pinching off any excess.
5. With both palms, gently pat the ball into a disk about 5 inches in diameter and ½ inch thick.
6. Cook pupusas on a flat griddle over medium-high heat about 4 minutes on each side, until lightly bronzed. Serve hot with tomato salsa and curtido salad (see box above).

## SCRAMBLED EGGS WITH FLOR DE IZOTE   Serves 4

### Ingredients
4 tablespoons olive oil
½ onion, diced
1 tomato, diced
1 chicken bouillon cube or sachet
4-6 eggs
1 teaspoon salt
Black pepper (to taste)
1 2-pound jar of flor de izote*, drained; or 1 pound fresh flor de izote (they do grow in Somerville gardens!)

### Directions
1. Heat oil in a large frying pan on medium-high and cook onion and tomato until soft, about 5 minutes.
2. Add chicken bouillon and stir.
3. Add flor de izote and stir; continue cooking for 5 minutes.
4. Add salt and black pepper, to taste and stir.
5. Beat the eggs in a bowl and pour slowly over the cooking flor de izote.
6. Gently stir until the eggs are cooked, about 5 more minutes. Serve hot with warm tortillas.

Caleb Cole

Rachel Strutt

Clockwise from top left: Shopping carts waiting to be filled at Market Basket; Rokeya Kabir and a ruhu fish from Bangladesh, at WellFoods Plus; spices at Pão de Açúcar; Journeyman's cured bluefish; Ronnie Saksua (of the former restaurant Ronnarong), who has participated in our Ginger Explosion! events; sopa azteca; part of the beer selection at Little India; a portrait of Antonella D'Eramo by Meagan O'Brien.

Dustin Kerstein

Caleb Cole

Dustin Kerstein

# Appetizers

 THE MULTIETHNIC MAGNET

 A FRUITFUL EXCHANGE

 JOURNEYMAN'S CURED BLUEFISH AND GOUGÈRES

 SRI LANKAN HOPPERS WITH MISO-GLAZED BARBECUED EGGPLANT

 SOPA AZTECA

 GINGER CHICKEN WINGS

Top left: Market Basket manager Mike Dunleavy; bottom right: Market Basket employee Felix Cabrera, who hails from Honduras.

# THE MULTIETHNIC MAGNET

**In Union Square, Market Basket lures crowds with bargains and batatas—*and* complements the neighborhood's smaller international food stores.**

Text by June Carolyn Erlick | Photography by Caleb Cole

The produce department at the Market Basket just outside Union Square reflects the diversity of the store's clientele: shoppers browse through daikon, chayote, ñame, eddoes, tomatillos and batatas, as well as a wide assortment of low-priced tomatoes, cucumbers, lettuce and other produce. Throughout the store, a poetic plethora of varied products—such as halawa, guarana, yerba mate, sofrito, polenta and potato gnocchi—awaits eager buyers.

Market Basket is nearly always full, but on a Saturday morning, the activity reaches a crescendo. A woman from Ghana and her 4-year-old daughter look over the root vegetables. A local musician who rehearses nearby buys flour to make a cake. Four Salvadoran shoppers compare cheese brands, while a lanky woman in a brightly flowered headscarf puts a jar of Marshmallow Fluff into her basket. Carts flood the aisles, and store staff with names as diverse as the shoppers are constantly stocking the shelves.

Devang Bhatt and his new wife, Lamisa Parkar, love Market Basket for its inexpensive produce. The couple shop here about every two weeks and also frequent Little India, a market next door. Here, the newlyweds, who live in Beacon Hill, can speak their native language with the shopkeepers. "We get anything and everything Indian, including spices, frozen Indian dishes, fresh produce, incense, Indian beers, Indian basmati rice," Bhatt explains. "Even though some of these items may be found in Market Basket, like rice, the brands we grew up with are seen only at Little India." He adds that certain spices, like turmeric and ginger powder, are much better here than the "generic, tasteless and nonfragrant" brands you find at supermarkets.

Like many who come to Union Square from Somerville and beyond, Bhatt and Parker are two-destination shoppers. Contrary to what one might think, the large supermarket serves as a magnet for local stores. Many shoppers visit Market Basket *and* their favorite ethnic store. Union Square, with more than a half dozen international markets ranging from Indian to Korean to Brazilian, offers rich opportunities for ethnic shoppers and adventurous cooks.

Countless Market Basket shoppers have discovered that shopping throughout Union Square can be an international culinary treasure hunt. "I just went to La Internacional for the first time and found the kind of Colombian chocolate you melt," says Rob Karl, a Princeton professor from the Boston area on sabbatical and living in Somerville. "Now that I'm back in the neighborhood, I go to Market Basket. I'd take the produce over Shaw's, and I've had luck with the meats. My sister even found Alpina Arequipe [a Colombian milk sweet similar to dulce de leche] there last month!"

Karl is lucky. He lives close enough to Market Basket that he doesn't have to jockey for a spot in the 203-car parking lot that's almost always full.

The Somerville store is one of 63 in the Massachusetts-based DeMoulas Market Basket chain, which, according to *Supermarket News*, is known for "high-volume sales and market-leading prices."

"We like to think our customer service is exceptional," says Somerville store director Mike Dunleavy, who has been at this location for 18

Byron Cabrera and his mother, Nora, the owners of La Internacional.

years. "We like to say hello, to thank customers for shopping here and to get the customers the products they want." He pays special attention to customer requests; new products are being added constantly, mostly on the basis of requests at the customer service department.

Dunleavy, who began his career with Market Basket in high school 33 years ago, says the store with its 350-400 employees attracts shoppers from Somerville, Cambridge, Arlington, Medford—and further—because it is the closest Market Basket to Boston.

Says Alysia Abbott, a Cambridge-based writer, "Market Basket is always a little insane and crowded—and there are so many choices. It makes me happy to be with people who are excited about getting such bargains."

Nora Cabrera, who owns La Internacional Food with her son Byron, says, "Many come for Market Basket and they come by here. Even if one wants to be American, you can't eat hamburgers and hot dogs all day long," she says, with an ample smile lighting up her face.

Cabrera's customers come from as far away as Brockton, Malden and Revere; many of her patrons are Haitian, but others hail from Brazil, Guatemala, El Salvador and Mexico. The shop also attracts American customers searching for unusual ingredients such as bottled loroco flowers and djon djon mushrooms, which are used by Haitian cooks to flavor rice.

Even though it's general retail wisdom that larger stores drive out smaller ones, James Tillotson, Tufts University professor of food policy and international business, says the supermarket magnet effect is not all that uncommon. The critical mass of markets—big and small—in Union Square attracts customers from a broad geographic area.

"Americans are very experimental in what they eat, and immigrants when they come to a strange land want the flavors from back home," Tillotson says. "People shop around. So if the supermarket and the specialty shop are serving different needs, shoppers might go to both."

In addition to food specialties, additional services such as phone cards and music or clothes from the home country might increase sales "if the services are done well," Tillotson adds.

One local store that offers such services is Pão de Açúcar, a Brazilian market that offers Brazilian DVDs, a fax service and key duplication. It also features a hot Brazilian buffet that fills the store with scents of freshly cooked dishes like feijoada.

"Our customers are 75 percent Brazilian, and they come from a distance—Allston, Lowell, even Connecticut," says owner Francisco Silva. "They usually go to Market Basket beforehand, but they come here to find something different, things they can't get at Market Basket." He stocks Brazilian herbs, cosmetics and soaps. Among his best-selling items are various brands of frozen pão de queijo, a Brazilian cheese bread made with manioc flour.

Rokeya Kabir, who owns WellFoods Plus with her husband, Jahangir.

Jahangir Kabir, who owns nearby WellFoods Plus with his wife, Rokeya, is proud of the fact that he can even beat out Market Basket in price on a few items. He holds up an 11-pound box of Medjool dates, which he sells for $43. "Come Ramadan, I sell mountains of these." His customers are originally from India, Pakistan, Nepal, Algeria, Indonesia, the Philippines and the United States and also include Kosher customers who purchase halal meat. Huge fish called lakka and an abundance of goat and other halal meat are among the specialty offerings not found in the neighboring supermarket.

Down the road at Market Basket, dinnertime shoppers are scooping up hot rotisserie chicken at $3.99. The loudspeaker announces a sale on boneless chuck steak at $2.99. Wilson Moreira, a casually dressed Somerville housepainter originally from Minas Gerais, Brazil, stands in the express line with three packages of frozen quail and six cans of coconut milk in his basket. The quail—which he doctors with Brazilian spices and liquid smoke–is for a barbecue tonight on his gas grill. The coconut milk is destined for his wife's birthday cake.

Moreira says he often visits smaller local markets, but tonight he's in a hurry. "That's the beauty of the express line!" he declares before darting out into the mayhem of the Market Basket lot.

—*June Carolyn Erlick, editor-in-chief of* ReVista, the Harvard Review of Latin America, *is the author of* Disappeared, A Journalist Silenced *and* A Gringa in Bogotá, Living Colombia's Invisible War. *A Somerville resident, she shops at Market Basket and several of the area's ethnic stores.* ●

Left: Dipti Mistri, who owns Little India with her husband, Umesh; right: produce at Market Basket.

# A FRUITFUL EXCHANGE

**Artist Meagan O'Brien gets people from around the globe gabbing about grub—by offering a portrait in exchange for a story.**

A recent Intercambio group, with members hailing from Peru, Brazil, Colombia, Chile, Spain and the United States, finished off the season with a potluck party. Artist Meagan O'Brien is at far left.

At Intercambio, the Somerville Arts Council's culture and language exchange program, conversation topics range from verb conjugation to Afro-Brazilian beats to *La Liga* soccer scores. Yet the most prevalent subject is—you guessed it—food. So we invited artist Meagan O'Brien to conduct her "Portrait for a Story" project with our multilingual group. In exchange for a story about food, Meagan sketched a portrait of each storyteller. It was a fruitful cultural exchange—and a perfect fit for Intercambio, which translates to "exchange" in both Spanish and Portuguese.

Not familiar with Intercambio? This program gives "gringos" an opportunity to gab in foreign tongues with folks from Brazil, Guatemala, Colombia, Haiti, Nepal—the list goes on. And it's also a chance for immigrants learning English at the Somerville Center for Adult Learning Experiences (our Intercambio partners) to chat with native English speakers. At each session we split up participants into pairs and spend half the time speaking English and half the time speaking another language; all participants are both students and teachers.

Beyond these food stories, many of the recipes and recipe introductions in this book come from our "intercambians." So we say: *gracias, obrigada* and *dhanyabaad*! *—Rachel Strutt*

Portraits, Interviews: Meagan O'Brien | Storytellers: Alexandre Carvalho, Ovidia Machorro, Antonella D'Eramo, Debra Olin, Len White | Translation help: Jennifer Carlson, Grace de Cunha, Marcelo Zicker

Storyteller: Alexandre Carvalho
Origin/Languages: São Paolo, Brazil/Portuguese; practices English at Intercambio
Union Square Recommendation: Chorizo a la Plancha con Yuca at Casa B

OK, this story is about making yucca flour. When I was 17, I went to Bahia with two of my cousins—we were all about the same age. Bahia is where my mom was born; we were going to stay with my great aunt. We had a vacation and wanted to go somewhere fun. Bahia is known for its beautiful beaches, so we said, "Let's go!"

When we got there, they told us, "Oh, this week we're going to go to the farm." Then they told us we'd be at the farm all week! And we said, "Seriously?"

When we got there, we learned there was no electricity, no hot water, no TV. Nothing. The next day at four in the morning, they woke us up. We thought, "What's going on?" They told us we were going to work and it was time to eat breakfast.

Then it was time to work. Other workers brought us the yucca roots from the fields. First we cut off the skin; then we used a crank to grind it all up. Next we had to strain the yucca with a kind of rag, to get all the liquid out. Then the mixture was sifted. Finally, there was a guy who dried the yucca on a flat slab—like a giant frying pan heated by a fire underneath. The guy pushed the yucca around until it dried and became flour.

Yucca flour is very popular in Brazil. My mother used to make the most delicious cake with yucca flour!

Anyway, that's what we did for the whole week: make yucca flour. It was unbelievably hot. From noon to three you can't work outside, especially in the summer. We would have lunch at noon, and then take a nap. At four, we would go to the lake and stay there until it got dark. The first day I hated it there. But then during the week, it started to feel really good. I wish I could go back there for another vacation.

Bem, esta história é sobre como é feita a farinha de mandioca. Quando eu tinha 17 anos, fui para a Bahia com dois dos meus primos, nós éramos todos da mesma idade. Bahia é o estado onde minha mãe nasceu; nós fomos para ficar na casa de uma tia. Nós estávamos de férias e queríamos ir para uma lugar onde pudéssemos se divertir. A Bahia é conhecida pelas lindas praias, então dissemos: vamos lá!

Quando chegamos lá , eles falaram para nós, "oh, esta semana nós vamos para a roça". Logo em seguida disseram que iríamos ficar a semana inteira! Então nos dissemos - sério?

Quando chegamos lá, vimos que não tinha energia, não tinha chuveiro e, não tinha TV. Nada. No dia seguinte, às 4hs da manhã, eles nos acordaram. Nós pensamos - o que esta acontecendo? Eles nos disseram que tínhamos que ir trabalhar e era a hora do café da manhã.

Então era hora de trabalhar. As pessoas que

começaram cedo chegaram com as mandiocas. Primeiro, nós tivemos que descascar todas as mandiocas, depois nós usamos um moedor para moer todas elas. A próxima etapa era tirar toda a água da mandioca, para isso, usamos um pano para torcer até ficar bem seca. Depois colocamos numa peneira. Finalmente, o último passo era secar a farinha no forno, que era uma chapa gigante de metal com fogo a lenha embaixo. Então um tipo mexia a farinha com um rodo de um lado para o outro até secar.

Farinha de mandioca é muito popular no Brasil, minha mãe costumava fazer uma torta deliciosa com a farinha de mandioca!

De uma forma ou de outra, isto foi o que fizemos durante toda semana: fizemos farinha de mandioca. Estava incrivelmente quente, por isso tínhamos que acordar cedo. Do meio dia até as 3hs não se pode trabalhar fora, especialmente no verão. Então nós tínhamos que almoçar ao meio dia e depois tirar um cochilo. Por volta das 4hs da tarde, íamos para um lago e ficávamos até escurecer. O primeiro dia eu

odiei, mas depois comecei a gostar e me senti bem estando lá. Eu desejo um dia voltar lá novamente de férias.

Storyteller: Len White

Origin/Languages: Cohasset, Massachusetts/ English; practices Portuguese at Intercambio

Union Square Recommendation: Saag Paneer at Union Square Pizza

I live pretty close to Union Square so I come here a lot. My original mission was to go to every restaurant in the square. One of the places lingering on my list a long time was Union Square Pizza, right next to El Potro. For the longest time I didn't go in there. Why? Because it looks like every other sub joint in the Boston area. The place almost has a retro charm, like a cute diner-type thing, but it's just too...not quite there.

OK, so this is what happens. I'm staring at the menu, looking for anything interesting—and it's cheese steak, pastrami, hamburger with fries, all the same sub food. This is stuff I like on occasion but, eh. Then I notice this woman below the menu who is clearly the proprietor. She's Indian, I think. She's wearing this beautiful flowing gown with designs you never see on a western piece of clothing.

Then I notice the TV is on behind me, and they're speaking what sounds like a Hindi language. OK, so I figure out this place is Indian. I look back at the menu and then finally ask the woman, "Do you have, uh, do you have Indian food?"

She then says, "What do you like?"

I responded, "Well, I love the bread—naan, but you need a special oven to…"

"We have that in the back," she responded. "What else do you want?"

"Well, how about chicken tikka masala with rice?" She says OK and I ask her if they really have the stuff to make that. She then hands me a full menu featuring Indian food! I've been there several times now, and taken friends. Their chicken tikka masala is pretty good, and the saag paneer is really good. It's still a bit of a mystery to me. I never really probe; I just call it the secret Indian joint.

Storyteller: Antonella D'Eramo

Origin/Languages: Metrowest Boston/English; practices Spanish at Intercambio

Union Square connection: "I go to Reliable Market for Asian food; Bloc 11 to study and for coffee; the Independent to eat and drink; Cantina La Mexicana for my Mexican fix—oh, and Midnight Market for scratch tickets!"

Growing up, until my grandfather passed away, my family jarred tomatoes for what seemed like the entire month of August—seriously. My grandfather's whole backyard was a garden where he only grew tomatoes. So, in August the tomatoes were ready and we went to work. After planting and caring for the tomatoes, my grandfather would go back to Capestrano in the Abruzzo region of Italy for a few months, so the ladies of the family were in charge of the picking and the jarring.

After picking the tomatoes from the garden, someone had to skin them and de-seed them. Then us kids had a lot of fun slamming them down in the jars with wooden spoons. We also added salt and fresh basil that was grown in the garden. And that was it! They all got boiled in a big kettle and were then sealed for winter. My mom, aunt and grandmother used the canned tomatoes for the rest of the year to make their homemade sauce.

I remember one August evening we had been jarring all day. We were covered in tomato sauce, having fun. Meanwhile our dog was running around the neighborhood and got sprayed by a skunk. So when he came back into the yard we took the excess juice from the tomatoes and poured it all over him instead of putting him in the bathtub with tomato juice—the usual remedy. Of course, what do dogs do when they get wet? They shake it off. So the whole yard—plus walls, patio and furniture—was covered in tomato sauce!

As teenagers the jarring wasn't as thrilling for my sisters and I—it was more of a chore. So we helped more sporadically. A few years ago I asked my mom, "So, how do I make tomato sauce?" because, silly me, over the years I never paid close attention. I asked, "What do I buy at the grocery store—crushed tomatoes, pulped tomatoes or whole tomatoes?" My mom couldn't tell me because she didn't know, she'd just always used the tomatoes she'd jarred.

Now my parents buy tomatoes at a farmers' market to make a few jars, but it's not the same. I told them I'd help this year if they'd give me a few jars—then I'll try making my mom's tomato sauce.

I do miss food from Guatemala. Everything is homemade there. If I cook for my kids here, they like tamales. Sometimes I make a lot and freeze them. Then, for days, it's like tamales, tamales, tamales!

Name: Ovidia Machorro
Origin/Languages: Livingston, Guatemala/Spanish; practices English at Intercambio
Union Square connection: Shops at Market Basket

Growing up, we made tamales for Christmas. Sometimes my mother would make 500 and we'd all help her. She had a little business to make some extra money and would sell them to people in the town during Christmastime, or a *novenario* [nine-day mourning period following a funeral]. It is a lot of work because we had to cook the corn first, then take the corn off the cob. Then we'd grind it in a *molino*. My mom used to put me on the molino; I would do it early in the morning before I went to school. Here you just go to a supermarket and buy cornmeal!

We cut the banana leaves down from the tree by tying a knife to a mop or broomstick. Then we burned them in a big fire to make them soft. Next, we peeled and washed them, then cut them into little pieces to wrap tamales. Inside the tamale we put the corn mixture and then chicken or pork and salsa—made with tomatoes, toasted sesame seeds, dried chili, black pepper, onions and garlic.

Si extraño mi comida de Guatemala porque todo es hecho en casa allí. Cuando cocino para mis hijos aquí, a ellos les gustan mucho los tamales. Los pongo en el freezer y ellos los comen casi todos los días.

En Guatemala nos gusta hacer los tamales para las Navidades. A veces mi mama hacía hasta 500 tamales y todos la ayudábamos. Tenía un pequeño negocio para ganar un poco más de dinero y vendía tamales a la gente del pueblo para la Navidad o los novenarios. Para hacer los tamales tiene mucho trabajo porque nosotros teníamos que cocinar el maíz y hacer la masa en el molino. Mi mama me ponía a mi en el molino antes de ir a la escuela. Aquí voy al supermercado a comprar la masa.

Cortábamos las hojas de banano del árbol, usábamos un palo de madera largo y poníamos un cuchillo en la punta. Después las cocíamos en un gran fuego para ablandarlas y las cortábamos en pedazos y las lavábamos para envolver cada tamal. Cada uno lleva harina de maíz y carne de pollo o de cerdo y salsa—se hace con tomates, chiles secos, ajonjolí tostado, pimienta negra, ajo, cebolla.

Storyteller: Deb Olin

Origin/Languages: Atlantic City, New Jersey/English practices Spanish at Intercambio

Union Square recommendation: "I am crazy about the Saturday morning farmers' market in Union Square. It's the best!"

OK. So. I'm going to tell you about the Granny Ethel cookies.

My grandmother came from Russia or Poland; we're not sure—during the time between the wars, borders kept changing. She made these cookies when we visited her. We called them Granny Ethel cookies. We've never known them by another name and I've never known anyone else who makes them.

They are similar to rugelakh, which are made with butter and are sold in some Jewish bakeries. My grandmother made her cookies with oil so, you know, there is a very different taste. As she got older I guess they got harder to make, so she didn't make them as much. One time I asked her if I could watch her make them, which I did. A few years went by and I asked her for the recipe. Do you think she had the recipe? No. She didn't have the recipe. She said, "Well, you put in some flour." And I said, "Well, how much flour?" Long pause. "Eh, I don't know...three cups of flour. Then you throw in some vanilla." I say, "How much vanilla?" She says, "Half an egg shell", and this is the way it went.

Then I tried to make them. I had many failed attempts, but over the years, as I experimented, I perfected the recipe. And now my grandmother is gone and I make them at Chanukah. I make them for my brother and his family and for my mother and my Uncle Harry. The special thing is—you know those tins that the Danish butter cookies come in? The cookies have to go in those tins because that's what you send them in. So Uncle Harry, after he's done with the tin, he puts a five dollar bill in it and mails it back to me—to ensure he'll get more.

I'm the only one who makes these cookies. My brother makes me swear I won't give anyone else the recipe. I don't know why. It's like I'm going to take the recipe to my grave. But the thing is, you have to watch them being made. You can't just give someone the recipe. ●

# CURED BLUEFISH AND GOUGÈRES

**A few bites into this pairing from Journeyman's chefs and, chances are, you will be a devotee of bluefish—not to mention fancy French cheesy puffs.**

Meg Grady-Troia, one of the co-owners of Journeyman, urges you to give bluefish a go.

Meg Grady-Troia, manager and co-owner of Journeyman, thinks bluefish has been getting a bad rap. So she and fellow co-owners/chefs Diana Kudajarova and Tse Wei Lim have come up with a bluefish recipe that will win over the taste buds of almost any eater. By first curing the fish, you infuse it with a complex, curious and—most important—delicious flavor.

Now, if you've only ever seen the word "cured" on the menu of a fancy restaurant, or heard one of the Food Network chefs toss it out casually, rest assured that the process is, in fact, both simple and fun. And although Meg suggests two aromatic blends with which to cure your fish, you can play around with flavor combinations to find the one that suits your palate and complements your meal.

But where to get your fish? The folks at Journeyman strive to source all the ingredients locally, and they would certainly encourage you to do the same. Try the Union Square Farmers' Market, to see whether Jordan Brothers Seafood has any fresh bluefish fillets. You could also try Market Basket or Courthouse Seafood in East Cambridge. Or, depending on where you live, ask your local fishmonger.

If you truly want to dazzle your guests, pair your bluefish with another Journeyman recipe: gougères. Serve these savory cheesy pastry puffs warm or cold, as an appetizer or a side. Follow the directions carefully and you'll end up with a pile of golf-ball-sized pastries with an airy, yet very flavorful, center. *Bon appétit*!

Recipe: Journeyman Restaurant | Text: Jarrett Lerner | Photography: Dustin Kerstein | Recipe Testing: Katherine Perry

# CURED BLUEFISH  Serves 4

## Ingredients

desired number of bluefish fillets
salt and sugar for seasoning
either: orange zest and fennel fronds

or: cracked white pepper,
coriander (toasted whole seeds)
and lemon zest

> **Recipe tip**: You can leave the bluefish pin bones in, though removing them may provide a more enjoyable eating experience. There are many videos online that offer great instruction on how to remove pin bones.

## Directions

1. Pull all pin bones out of the fillet, but leave the skin on.
2. Mix together equal parts salt and sugar by weight.
3. Mix together the aromatics you want to use—either the cracked white pepper, coriander and lemon zest, or the orange zest and fennel fronds
4. Rub a generous amount of the salt and sugar mixture on the flesh side of the fillet.
5. Sprinkle on the aromatics of your choice.
Note: The layer of curing mixture should be a 1/4 inch thick and completely cover the fish, so that the flesh is no longer visible. If you have more than one piece of bluefish, you can stack them, flesh sides together.

6. Wrap the fish in plastic.
7. Prepare it for curing by placing it in a glass baking dish or a similar container made of nonreactive material. Put a smaller dish on top and weigh it down with about 5 pounds of weight (canned goods work well, or 2 bricks).
8. Refrigerate for 48 to 72 hours, taking the bluefish out every 12 hours to flip it. Do not drain off the liquid.
9. After 48 to 72 hours, unwrap the fillets, rinse off the remaining cure under cold water and pat dry.
10. Thinly slice fillets crosswise at a 45-degree angle, and store in the fridge wrapped in plastic until ready to serve.

# GOUGÈRES   Makes 20

## Ingredients

1 cup water

7 tablespoons butter

1 cup flour

5 eggs

3 ounces grated Gruyère

1 tablespoon salt

a pinch of sugar

optional: 2 ounces additional grated Gruyère for topping

**Recipe tip**: Gougères freeze very well. If freezing, pipe dough onto a parchment-lined baking sheet (you can pipe them close together if not freezing) and put in freezer. Transfer the gougères to a more convenient container once they are fully frozen. Bake them whenever you want—they still taste great—but remember that they'll take a minute or two longer to bake than if not frozen.

## Directions

1. Preheat oven to 450ºF.

2. Prepare a baking sheet lined with parchment paper.

3. In a pot, mix together the water, butter, salt, and sugar.

4. Bring mixture to a boil.

5. Turn down the heat and pour in the flour, mixing vigorously with a wooden spoon as you go. The mixture will quickly come together in a ball.

6. When the dough begins to smell like a biscuit and leaves a sticky film on the bottom of the pot—this will happen quickly!—tip it out into the bowl of a standing mixer.

7. Beat the dough with a paddle at low speed for about 30 seconds to let the dough cool a little.

8. Add the eggs, one at a time. The dough will break when you add each egg, then come together into a cohesive mass. Once this happens, you can add another egg.

9. Once all 5 eggs have been integrated into the dough, scrape down the bowl, restart the mixer, and add the Gruyère until it's also integrated (this will happen quickly).

10. Transfer the dough to a piping bag and pipe your gougères onto the parchment-lined baking sheet into mounds. The size is up to you—slightly larger than a quarter is traditional. Make sure to leave at least 1.5 inches of space between each gougère.

11. If you'd like, you can add a little tuft of the grated Gruyère on top of each gougère.

12. Bake for 7–8 minutes, or until the gougères are a crispy, golden brown on the outside and the centers are hollow but still moist.

# SRI LANKAN HOPPERS WITH MISO-GLAZED BARBECUED EGGPLANT

**The woman who dreamed up the Arts Council's Hungry Tiger Street Food Festival brings a bit of Southeast Asia to your table.**

Mary Goodman displaying a crosshatch-cut eggplant.

I have been working, studying and trekking around Asia since 2005. There is so much I love over there, but more than anything, I am captivated by the night markets, with their exotic eats and atmospheric allure. They can be found everywhere in Southeast Asia, from cities like Taipei and Mandalay to sleepy little fishing villages. Some favorites include the world famous ShiLin Night in Taipei, and some little fly-by-night shindig in Rayong, Thailand, where I first tasted fried grasshoppers.

So, when I team up with the Arts Council to throw the Hungry Tiger Street Food Festivals, we try to capture some of the flavor of Southeast Asian markets. These markets take place at night and include wandering musicians, unusual craft vendors and fire artists.

Back to Asia. Of course every region has its distinctive foods, yet Southeast Asian cities also offer epically diverse cuisine—a bit like Union Square! While studying Thai massage in Chiang Mai, Thailand, I found myself sampling myriad cuisines: Burmese, German, Pakistani, Nepalese and more. Sri Lankan hoppers pop up again and again in my travels. A common Sri Lankan dish, these crêpe-like treats can envelope a variety of fillings: sweet, savory or spicy.

This particular hopper recipe is gluten free, nut free, vegan—and delicious. If you want to really make people swoon, drizzle the hoppers with Kewpie mayonnaise and then sprinkle them with gomasio (a dry condiment made with unhulled sesame seeds).

Recipe & Text: Mary Goodman | Photography: Dustin Kerstein | Recipe Testing: Katherine Perry

# SRI LANKAN HOPPERS (SRI LANKAN CRÊPES) Serves 4

## Ingredients

2 teaspoons instant yeast granules
1 tablespoon sugar
⅛ cup lukewarm water (100 to 110°F, should feel
  warm but not hot on your wrist)
4 cups rice flour*
1 cup lukewarm water (add a bit more water if needed)
1 cup lukewarm beer
1 13-ounce can of coconut milk mixed with ½ cup of
  lukewarm water
2 tablespoons sugar
canola oil (to oil the wok)
salt to taste

## Directions

1. First, make the yeast mixture: mix first 3 ingredients, and leave for 10-15 minutes until frothy. If the mixture is not frothy, the yeast was too old, or water was not the right temperature.
2. Put the rice flour in a large bowl and add the yeast mixture. Next add 1 cup of water and 1 cup of beer. Mix until smooth.
3. Cover the bowl with a wet cloth or plastic wrap; leave for about eight hours in a warm place. The batter should rise to double in size.
4. Next, add three-quarters of the coconut milk-and-water mixture and 2 tablespoons sugar; stir well. If mixture is too thick, add more liquid. The batter should be thinner than pancake batter. Add salt to taste.
5. Heat a small wok or 8-inch nonstick skillet on medium. Wipe the pan down with an oil-soaked towel. Add about ¼ cup of the batter to the pan and turn the pan in a circular motion so that the batter sticks to the sides, to make the bowl-like shape.
6. Cover and cook for about 2-3 minutes on low-medium heat, until the hopper is golden brown and crispy and the sides start to pull away. The hoppers should hold their own shape and peel off quite easily. You can use a butter knife to loosen it and shake it out of the pan.

**Tip**: You can crack an egg atop a hopper immediately after covering the sides of the pan to make a classic Sri Lankan breakfast!
***Shopping tip**: Mary suggests Mochiko brand, found at Reliable Market and other Asian markets.

# MISO-GLAZED BARBECUED EGGPLANT  Serves 4

*Shopping Tip: Find these ingredients at Reliable Market and other Asian markets.

## Ingredients

3 Japanese eggplants*

½ teaspoon sea salt

¼ teaspoon red chili flakes

3 tablespoons miso paste (Shiro, brown rice, or other mellow/light/sweet miso)*

¼ cup Thai red curry paste*

1½ teaspoon palm sugar (dark brown sugar can also be used)

2 sprigs cilantro, roughly chopped

optional: Kewpie mayonnaise and gomasio, for garnish*

## Directions

1. Preheat oven to broil.

2. Combine chili flakes, miso, red curry, and palm sugar to make an even paste.

3. Cut the eggplants in half. Score the cut sides in a cross-hatch pattern, and season with salt. Lightly grease a baking dish and place the eggplant halves in it cut side up; broil for 5 minutes.

4. Remove eggplant from the oven, spread the paste on the eggplants evenly, and return to the broiler for another 2½ to 3 minutes. Transfer to a serving platter and garnish with chopped cilantro. If using Kewpie mayonnaise and gomasio, sprinkle on cilantro last.

# SOPA AZTECA

**This recipe has inspired curious cooks to explore the exotic flavors of Mexico—and the many wonders of local markets.**

Rachel Strutt (far right) leads a market tour; here the group discusses the medicinal qualities of bitter melon at Little India.

Over the past seven years, Arts Council staffers like myself have led gaggles of inquisitive foodies on tours of Union Square's international markets. We pop into places like New Bombay and Casa de Carnes, chat with store owners and graze happily along the way. Tourgoers often try new products and pass them around—seaweed-wrapped rice crackers, Hello Kitty mango marshmallows, rajgira chikki (amaranth brittle) and more. Sometimes store owners give out samples, like Francisco Silva at Pão de Açúcar, who often passes around cups of Guaraná, a highly caffeinated soda flavored with Amazonian berries—think Brazilian Red Bull.

The goal of these tours is to broaden cultural understanding and encourage food tourism, and it appears to be working. Tourgoers usually buy items at each market, and Dipti Mistri of Little India reports that she sees many return customers. On these tours we often hand out recipes—like this one for Sopa Azteca—which feature exotic ingredients found in the markets we visit.

So, about this soup. The history of Sopa Azteca is murky, yet one fact is clear—whether it was the Aztecs or a more recent people, the inventors of this soup knew what they were doing. With its piquant broth, tortilla crunch and soft chunks of avocado and cheese, the soup is a delicious study in contrasts.

These days, Sopa Azteca is a staple throughout Mexico, where recipes vary slightly by region. In Guanajuato, they use guajillo peppers; in Oaxaca, they use pasilla peppers. In our recipe, we use dried pasilla peppers—their earthy flavor lends a delicious complexity to this soup. Another ingredient is epazote, an herb used by the Aztecs and still common in Mexican cuisine. If they're out of it at La Internacional, ask the friendly owners to order some. And in the meantime, the soup still tastes *muy rico* without it.

Recipe and Text: Rachel Strutt | Photography: Bess Paupeck (this page); Dustin Kerstein (next page) | Recipe Testing & Food Styling: Heather Balchunas

# SOPA AZTECA (TORTILLA SOUP) Serves 4

## Ingredients

8 plum tomatoes or 5 regular tomatoes, cut in halves

1 medium white onion, thinly sliced

3 garlic cloves, peeled

approximately 2 tablespoons vegetable or olive oil,
   plus oil for frying tortillas

2 large dried pasilla chilies*

3 cups chicken broth

1 tablespoon dried, chopped epazote leaves*

*Shopping tip: Available at La Internacional and other Latino markets.

2 dried avocado leaves (or bay leaves)*

corn tortillas*

1 avocado, pitted, flesh scooped out, cut into small cubes

1 cup chopped queso fresco* (or use a mild feta)

optional: Mexican crema*, chopped cilantro
   and lime wedges, for garnishes

## Directions

1. Roast tomatoes, onion and whole garlic cloves on a grill; or in an oven with a little olive oil at 400 degrees. (Roast until garlic is fork tender; cover with foil if necessary).

2. Meanwhile, toast chilies in a small dry pan on medium heat, for 2 minutes each side; do not burn. Then devein and deseed the chilies (or leave in some seeds if you like it spicy). Next, add chili pieces to a pan of boiling water (use just enough water to cover chilies). Soak for a few minutes to soften.

3. Add chilies to a blender and purée.

4. Next add roasted onions and garlic and purée. Then add tomatoes and purée.

5. Add 1 tablespoon olive oil to a large pan and heat. Add tomato mixture and boil for 5 minutes; the mixture will reduce. Then add chicken stock, epazote and avocado leaves (or bay leaves) and cook on low for 15 minutes. Add salt to taste—go easy if stock is salty. Remove avocado leaves or bay leaves.

6. Cut several tortillas into strips and fry in about a half inch of vegetable oil until golden brown. Remove with tongs and place on a paper towel.

7. In a bowl, arrange pieces of avocado, cheese and tortilla strips. Pour the broth over these ingredients.

If you like, garnish with Mexican crema, cilantro and a lime wedge.

# GINGER CHICKEN WINGS

**A food entrepreneur and an up-and-coming chef get worked up about a certain tuber.**

Will Gilson (left) and Aaron Cohen often team up to produce offbeat foodie events, like Ginger Explosion!, part of the Arts Council's ArtsUnion series.

I run Eat Boston, an outfit that organizes food events, like Ice Cream Showdowns, Beer and Bacon Festivals and pop-up restaurant nights, in unlikely locations, including a hair salon and the British Consulate. I often throw these events in Union Square—at places like the Taza Chocolate factory and Bloc 11 Cafe—for one main reason: I live here. Convenience aside, it's a friendly locale for the types of events I put together; there are several great restaurants and it is one of the best food-shopping neighborhoods in the city.

Over the years, I have hosted several Ginger Explosion! events in Union Square that feature the best ginger dishes local chefs have to offer. Guests also receive a ginger cocktail made with Domaine de Canton ginger liqueur to wash it all down. Ginger is an explosive little tuber, yet it can also be versatile and subtle and works well in all kinds of dishes, from sweet to spicy to savory. These chicken wings from Chef Will Gilson of Bridgestreet in Inman Square are no exception.

Gilson, who has been cheffing it up since he was a teenager on his dad's farm (now known as the Herb Lyceum at Gilson's), says, "People sometimes look down on a chicken dish, but an excellent barometer of a restaurant and a chef's talent is the chicken dish they have on the menu. If it's good, you can assume the rest of the dishes will be too. Besides, at barbecues and picnics, chicken will please most everyone (except for vegetarians, of course). Adding ginger to your standard picnic wings is a good way to punch up your offering and stand out from the run-of-the-mill BBQ wing crowd."

Text: Aaron Cohen | Recipe: Will Gilson | Food Styling, Photography & Recipe Testing: Rachel Blumenthal

# GINGER CHICKEN WINGS
Makes 25-30 wings

## Ingredients

1 cup honey

1 tablespoon sriracha hot sauce

¾ cup soy sauce or tamari

¼ cup minced garlic (8 to 12 cloves)

½ cup peeled and grated fresh
  ginger root

3 pounds chicken wings

¼ cup chopped scallions

**Tip**: Sriracha hot sauce also fires up Vietnamese noc cham (a dipping sauce and salad dressing) and works wonders mixed with mayo on sandwiches. Find it at Market Basket, Reliable Market and other Asian markets.

## Directions

1. Cook the honey, soy sauce, garlic, hot sauce, and ginger root in a small saucepan over low heat until the honey is melted.

2. Arrange the chicken meaty side down in 1 layer in a shallow baking pan and pour on the sauce. Cover the pan tightly with aluminum foil. Marinate overnight in the refrigerator.

3. Preheat the oven to 350°F.

4. Place the baking pan in the oven and bake for 30 minutes.

5. Uncover the pan, turn the chicken pieces over and raise the temperature to 375°F. Continue baking for 20 minutes or until the juices run clear and the sauce is a rich, dark brown.

6. Toss cooked wings with the scallions.

Caleb Cole

Rachel Blumenthal

Clockwise from top left: the staff at Cantina La Mexicana includes, from left to right, Mexico natives Abelardo Beiza, Carolina Rendón, Graciela Cortez and El Salvador native Armando Blanco; a tiella di Gaeta awaiting its top crust, Maria Curtatone slides a tiella into the oven; spicy coconut curried goat stew; Rabindra Lamichhane of New Bombay market; Francisco de la Barra's spice portrait of Sheila Borges of the Neighborhood Restaurant; ingredients that will find their way into a Haitian meal.

Dustin Kerstein

Rachel Strutt

Rachel Blumenthal

Dustin Kerstein

# Entrees

 LATIN FLAVOR

 PAINTING WITH PAPRIKA

 NEPALI KIDNEY BEAN CURRY, PULAO & TOMATO TIMUR PICKLE

 OKRA ETOUFFÉE, RIZ AU DJON DJON & FRIED PLANTAINS

 TIELLA DI GAETA

 SPICY COCONUT CURRIED GOAT STEW

# LATIN FLAVOR

**Union Square's Latino restaurant owners spice up the culinary landscape, share their native cultures—and fire up the local economy.**

Text by Rachel Strutt | Photography by Caleb Cole

*"¡Ponle más salsa güey, ándale! ¡Mi abuela es más rápida que tú!"* This roughly translates to, "I need more salsa man, c'mon! My grandmother is faster than you!" It's the sort of kitchen banter you might overhear in many Union Square restaurants.

Restaurant kitchens can be great places to practice a foreign language, whether it's Spanish, Portuguese or Haitian Kreyol. You'll pick up culinary lingo and some delicious slang as well. Throughout the country it is common to find immigrants, especially Latinos, working in kitchens as prep cooks, line cooks and dishwashers—the unsung heroes of the restaurant business. Union Square exemplifies this trend. Step into the heat of many Union Square kitchens—whether it's La Cantina Mexicana, the Irish-owned Independent or the Korean restaurant Buk Kyung—and you'll find yourself among Salvadorans, Mexicans, Brazilians and Peruvians, among others, slicing, sautéing and spinning plates toward hurried servers.

Yet the Latinos of Somerville's culinary scene don't just work tucked away in the kitchen. In the case of Union Square, they own restaurants—lots of them. Lima native Rosy Cerna owns two Peruvian restaurants; the Mexican-American Rendón family owns Cantina La Mexicana; and the Interiano family, originally from El Salvador, owns El Potro. There's also Casa B, owned by husband-and-wife Alberto Cabré and Angelina Jockovich, who hail from Puerto Rico and Colombia, respectively. And lest we forget, Ebi Sushi is owned by Adolfo and José Garcia, who come from Guatemala and craft Tekka Maki rolls that would make a Tokyo sushi master proud. In addition, two South American natives have opened cafés recently: Cafe Tango, owned by Argentinean Vicky Magaletta, and Fortissimo, owned by Brazilian Vinny Soares.

At these eateries, the owners and their family members also work as chefs, head cooks and managers. They are hands-on, and their personalities imbue their businesses with warm Latino flavor. Step into La Cantina and Roberto Rendón might greet you with a boisterous "Hola, gringa!" followed by "Have you tried my jalepeño margaritas?" A few doors down at Casa B, Jockovich will chat with you unhurriedly at the door, while downstairs, head chef Cabré is likely dazzling patrons at the kitchen bar by constructing one of his artful desserts. At El Potro on weekend evenings, Elias Interiano might just saunter up to your table and serenade you with his mariachi band.

Rosy Cerna, owner of Machu Picchu.

**Beyond generating food tourism, Union Square's restaurant owners create jobs. Collectively, the square's Latino-American restaurant owners employ about 60 people.**

None of these restaurateurs went to business school, and with the exception of Cabré of Casa B, none went to culinary school, either. Most worked their way up the restaurant ranks. Take, for example, Rosy Cerna, owner of two Union Square restaurants: Machu Picchu Restaurante Túristico and Machu Picchu Charcoal Chicken and Grill. Cerna came to Somerville from Lima, Peru, in 1995, speaking little English. Her first job was at Pentimento, a Cambridge restaurant that is now closed.

"I started doing prep work, then I moved into the kitchen," she explains. "Then I became cashier, then hostess, then waitress. I learned a lot. If there was something I didn't know how to do, I'd ask. I never said no! I always said, 'I can do this!' Everything I did there, I did with passion. I feel so grateful to the owners of that restaurant; they gave me the opportunity to move from one position to another."

Five years later, Cerna decided to buy Taco Loco in Union Square. Originally she planned to continue with the same name and menu. "At Taco Loco, I always wanted to do more," she recalls. " But because I'm not Mexican, I didn't know how to make more dishes. So after a while, I decided to do Peruvian because that's what I know. I was so afraid at first. I thought, people don't know about Peruvian food! I was worried I would have an empty restaurant." More than 10 years later, Cerna owns three restaurants in the city—including Mixtura on Beacon Street—and employs a total of 20 people.

El Potro owner Elias Interiano, who hails from Agua Caliente, El Salvador, worked his way up the ranks at various restaurants, first in Florida, then in Massachusetts. He opened El Potro in 2006. As he sees it, this path to restaurant ownership has big advantages. "If you get into the restaurant business and you don't have the experience—you don't know how to do everything yourself—you might as well not get into it," says Interiano with irresistible swagger. "Here I work in the front of the house, and I can go back to the kitchen and cook and wash dishes. It's the same. I can do it all."

Of course, there are other entrepreneurs who have opened markets, restaurants and bars in Union Square. Many were born in this country, yet the vast majority were born abroad, coming from such countries as Ireland, Portugal, Thailand and India. Even some franchises in the square are owned by immigrants: Subway, for example, is owned by Binoj Pradhan, from Nepal.

Collectively, the square's restaurateurs are fueling the local economy. "Diversity of choices in the food marketplace can contribute to the perception that a district is hot," says Brad Rawson, senior planner for

José García of Ebi Sushi presents a plate of a caterpillar sushi rolls.

the city's Office of Strategic Planning and Community Development. "That's what's happening in Union Square. What's more, if you can't get a table at one restaurant, you go somewhere else. Overall, you enjoy the culture and physical environment of the square; this may bring you back next week, to try some new exotic place. It helps everyone's bottom line."

Beyond generating food tourism, Union Square's restaurant owners create jobs. Collectively, the square's Latino-American restaurateurs employ about 60 people. Often, these owners employ relatives and Spanish-speaking people from cultures similar to their own, but not always. Casa B employs people from the United States, Mexico, Venezuela and Greece. José García of Ebi Sushi, who worked his way up the restaurant ladder at various Japanese establishments, employs a staff from Japan, China and Russia. "It's nice to give other people a chance," says García. "If my old boss did it for me, why wouldn't I do it for someone else?"

The food industry has long been a path for immigrants to enter the American economy and community. As García sees it, immigrants—often Latinos—take low-level restaurant positions because others won't.

"Why are there Latinos in the kitchen?" he asks rhetorically. "Because nobody else wants to do it. You have to work really hard. You have to work 60 to 70 hours a week. Some people work in kitchens because they don't have a choice. They might not love it but they have to send money to their countries."

Carolina Rendón, who owns Union Square's Cantina La Mexicana with her husband, Roberto, exemplifies this work ethic well. A native of San Luis Potosí, Mexico, Carolina emigrated to a small town near Brownsville, Texas, at age 17. There, she worked as a maid and met Roberto. The Rendóns settled in Somerville in 1988 and opened La Taqueria Mexicana in 1995. Carolina had worked for a few years at Boca Grande in Cambridge, but the couple had no experience running a restaurant of their own. It was a risk.

Yet immigrants, who have already risked leaving their homeland to start afresh in a new country, are familiar with risk. This is likely one reason—among many—why in every U.S. census since 1880, foreign-born Americans have been more likely to be self-employed than those born here.

Early on, Carolina recalls, it was tough. "We bought used clothes, we didn't go out to dinner. We didn't have a choice," she says. "Because I'm from Mexico, you keep going, you don't give up. I was nervous in the beginning. But my daughter had a friend at school whose family was from Portugal. They started a food business and were successful. I thought it was just us Latinos who did this, but I learned it was other people too. This made me feel more confident."

Carolina Rendón of Cantina La Mexicana.

By building successful restaurants, the Rendóns and the square's other immigrant food entrepreneurs have immersed themselves in the American economic landscape. Yet through food, these restaurateurs are also preserving their cultural customs.

At Cantina La Mexicana, for example, you'll find Enchiladas Potosinas, a specialty of San Luis Potosí, the state where Rosy Rendón grew up. You'll also taste many dishes spiced with chili piquin, which grew in abundance around her childhood home.

Downstairs at Casa B, Alberto Cabré sits below a series of old family portraits—black-and-white photographs taken when he was a child in Rio Piedras, Puerto Rico. "These are all real photos! They are not fake families!" jokes Alberto, who creates food inspired by Spanish, Caribbean and Colombian cuisine. "My food is very rooted in culture," he continues. "I like to reinterpret traditional dishes, so I'll take street food, for example, and make it high-end."

To illustrate his point, he talks about Casa B's Bacalaitos Fritos: salted cod fritters served with brandade and cilantro aioli. "When I was a little kid, we often spent weekends in Loíza, on the northeast coast of the island. We'd go to a little street vendor who sold great salted cod fritters. So I took these and made them my own. I added more puff, with baking powder. Then I added a French brandade spread on top, plus a little cilantro aioli. It's a high-end dish, but when people from Puerto Rico come here, they say, 'Oh my God, these are just like the fritters in Loíza!'"

"Food is one of the longest-lasting cultural norms that an immigrant group will bring," says Beth Forrest, a Somerville resident who teaches culinary history at the Culinary Institute of America in Hyde Park, New York. "You stop wearing the clothing, you stop speaking the language, but the last piece of culture to remain is foodways. Speaking for myself, I don't know any Polish folk dances, I don't speak Polish, but we still have pierogies at Thanksgiving."

Machu Picchu's Rosy Cerna supports this theory. "My American-born son says to me, 'Mommy, don't you get tired eating Peruvian food all the time?' I tell him I was born with this. I can't stop eating my food! Food is a strong connection. When I have my soup, Caldo de Gallina, made with eggs, chicken, pasta, and potato, I remember my mom making this soup back in Peru."

It seems that soup has a powerful way of triggering memories. Cerna also mentions Aguadito de Pollo, a chicken soup seasoned with ají amarillo—Peru's favorite pepper—and carbed up with potatoes and rice. Back in Peru, this hearty number is a popular hangover cure. "After too much drinking, this soup can revive the dead," she says. "If a Peruvian comes in here and sees it on the menu, it reminds them of home."

The food of immigrant restaurateurs entices not only their fellow expats, but gringos as well. Owners say that appealing to locals is crucial for success. Yet beyond the bottom line, Latino restaurant owners act as cultural ambassadors, some more intentionally than others.

For Cerna, the role of ambassador is one she takes seriously. At Machu Picchu Restaurante Turístico, diners can try dishes from throughout her native Peru, a country with diverse culinary influences, ranging from Japanese to Spanish. "I try to represent the main dishes from each of Peru's 20 states," she says. "On the menu, I explain where dishes come from. I love it when people come here and want to learn about a new culture. If somebody doesn't have the chance to go to Peru, they can come here and taste Peru."

Food is also entertwined with broader cultural traditions, like music. At restaurants in Peru, Mexico and El Salvador, you'll often find bands playing—and many of the square's restaurant owners bring this tradition to Somerville. Fridays at Machu Picchu, you'll catch an Andean band. Most Friday and Saturday nights at El Potro, owner Elias Interiano dons a spectacular pair of mariachi pants, picks up his accordian, and performs with his band, Estampa Mariachi de America.

Elias Interiano, owner of El Potro, with his son and restaurant manager, Jason.

"Mariachi is from Mexico," says Interiano, who started playing music in church as a young boy with his father. "But in Mexico and all of Central America, we all listen to the same kind of music. You can find a mariachi band in any corner of El Salvador. We are an authentic mariachi band, but we also mix in a little cumbia and bolero. I wanted to bring something to the square different from everyone else, something that represents our culture."

On a recent Friday evening at El Potro, the crowd is mixed; you can discern this by a quick assessment of facial hair. Several young Salvadoran men sitting at the bar have impeccably manicured mustaches. In stark contrast, several thickly bearded hipsters sit in a booth swilling Coronas.

Interiano's son, Jason, a remarkably poised 17-year-old who manages the restaurant, says this mix is the norm. "We have customers from all different cultures," he explains. "Everyone is welcome. At around 5 o'clock, you might have more customers of European or Asian descent. But later, towards 9 or 10, that's when the Hispanic population likes to go out. But there's nearly always a mix."

This mix of diners is typical throughout Union Square—and different from Davis Square, which draws a more affluent and homogenous dining crowd, and East Somerville, where you're likely to find fewer gringos. The mix reflects Union Square's broad range of food businesses coupled with a diverse yet increasingly gentrified residential landscape. But it's not just locals grazing at the square's eateries. Drawn by the promise of an "authentic" ethnic food experience—fueled hugely by Yelp, Chowhound and the foodie-crazed blogosphere—diners from the greater Boston area also are discovering Union Square.

Cerna says that her American customers, an estimated 50 percent of her clientele from throughout the

> **"They even order guinea pig! We only have it occasionally, for Mother's Day, for example, when it's a Peruvian tradition. But Americans will come in here specifically asking for guinea pig!"**

Boston area, are not looking to play it safe. "Americans order anything, including anticuchos, which are beef hearts," she says. "They love it! They even order guinea pig! We only have it occasionally, for Mother's Day, for example, when it's a Peruvian tradition. But Americans will come in here specifically asking for guinea pig! I am so surprised!"

Gastronomic diversity—including grilled guinea pig—is putting Union Square on the map. Hooray for food tourism! Yet this success comes with risks too. Might increased dining crowds and a growing number of upscale restaurants inadvertently threaten the neighborhood's delicious diversity? As the area gentrifies, might the smaller ethnic eateries and markets get pushed out—along with a more diverse clientele?

Elias Interiano, for one, is not worried. He says, "It's only going to get better. I feel we all should work together. Nobody takes anyone's business. You have a beer at one place, then go next door and have an enchilada. No matter how many businesses come to the square, it's actually good for all of us."

Similarly, Casa B's Alberto Cabré believes the current restaurants and markets complement each other. "I think we can coexist," he says. "There are times to eat in a high-end restaurant and times not to eat in a high-end restaurant. Chefs, for example, don't always want something fancy—I know I don't. I like going to Machu Picchu on the corner and having some grilled chicken. As far as the markets go, when I run out of stuff I go to La Internacional to buy plantains and avocados. For me it's a real benefit to have a Latino market around."

**As the area gentrifies, might the smaller ethnic eateries and markets get pushed out—along with a more diverse clientele?**

Whether or not Union Square can maintain its diversity in the long run, one thing is clear. Again and again, the square's Latino restaurant owners say that they feel welcome and supported here.

"I love Guatemala, but this is where I want my kids to grow up," says José García. "The American people are so nice. And the city has been very supportive." He pauses, then adds, "There is so much happening in Union Square right now. We have everything—Japanese, American, Mexican, tapas, sushi. I feel proud to be here."

Perhaps it's because this immigrant business group feels welcome that they, in turn, are so welcoming towards others—regardless of ethnicity, class or facial hairstyle.

Carolina Rendón sums up the square's Latino hospitality well. Recounting how she grew up in a small Mexican village just off the highway, not far from Ciudad Valles, she says her family often took in weary travelers en route to further destinations. "That's kind of what we do at La Taqueria. We like to make people feel at home."

*—Rachel Strutt is the program manager at the Somerville Arts Council. She hopes to one day speak Spanish as well as Union Square's Latino-American restaurant owners speak English.* ●

The cheery interior of El Potro; owner Elias Interiano imported these painted chairs from Guadalajara, Mexico.

# PAINTING WITH PAPRIKA

**An artist creates portraits of Union Square restaurant owners and chefs, incorporating spices within his paints.**

This portrait of Rungnapa Otero of Sweet Ginger incorporates soy flower, ginger, pepper and curry powder.

Globetrotting artist Francisco de la Barra recently painted a series of portraits of Union Square chefs and restaurant workers as part of the Somerville Arts Council's ArtsUnion initiative. He interviewed each subject—asking them about spices they like to use—and then incorporated those spices within his portraits. We recently caught up with de la Barra, a former Somerville Arts Council board member originally from Santiago, Chile, and asked him a series of questions about his project.

A spice portrait of Mario Borges of the Neighborhood Restaurant.

**Nibble: How do you think spices reflect the culture of Union Square?**

**Francisco de la Barra:** Spices are everywhere in the square, with so many Asian and Latin American restaurants—and all the international markets. In a way, spice is a marker of foreigners coming into the States, as their food tends to be spicier than American food.

**Nibble: Which were your favorite spices to work with and why did they work well?**

**Francisco:** Turmeric and annatto. They have strong colors, fine textures and lasting effects.

**Nibble: When you met with your portrait subjects and asked them about spices they use, how did they respond?**

**Francisco:** The response was actually very mild and matter-of-fact. For them spice is second nature—like butter and milk for us Westerners. At the same time, they were puzzled—like, why are you doing this?

**Nibble: How would you direct a newcomer to Union Square when it comes to the area's spicescape? Are there certain stores, restaurants and dishes you would recommend?**

**Francisco:** I would visit the markets first and then the restaurants. In this way, you can interact with the origin of food and then experience spice *in* the food, for a deeper cultural understanding. Usually in the markets, you get a more raw sense of the culture. The people who run markets tend to speak less English than the people who run a restaurant. New Bombay Market and La Internacional are my favorites, and I think, the most typical markets. I get turmeric from New Bombay Market and annatto from La Internacional. For restaurants, my favorites are Cantina la Mexicana and Sweet Ginger—I love their dishes with wide noodles, like pad see ew.

**Nibble: Your most recent work is very textural. Did working with spices have any lasting influences on your work?**

**Francisco:** More recently, I have used clay, ashes and coal. So yes, the sense of texture has lasted—that was the reason I used spices. Although not as organic as spices, my new mediums also convey a sense of nature. Yet whereas the spice portraits had a very tactile quality, the material I use now is more finely grained.

**Nibble: I understand a mouse once nibbled into one of your spice paintings?**

**Francisco:** Yes, after the chef portraits, I did a series of spice paintings depicting homeless people. At that time, I was also using seeds. I did a portrait of a guy wearing a white sweater made of white sesame seeds. The mouse ate the sweater completely—it disappeared! After that I learned that painting with paprika, turmeric and chili is fine, but seeds are problematic. I loved that the mouse ate the sweater, though. It gave the work a new dimension. ●

# NEPALI KIDNEY BEAN CURRY, PULAO & TOMATO TIMUR PICKLE

**This meal is both exotic and satisfying—plus, the timur will make your tongue tingle!**

Bimala (left) and Sabrina Thapa at Bombay Market.

This trio of vegan recipes come to us from Bimala Thapa, a Katmandu native who moved to Union Square with her family in 2005. Bimala says that back in Katmandu, she could see Mount Everest from her kitchen window on a clear day. Although she no longer has that view, Bimala still can find Nepali ingredients like timur (Szechuan pepper) and sweet lapsi (dried hog plum) by visiting the Nepali-owned New Bombay Market in Union Square—and on the way home, she can glance up at one of Somerville's towering peaks: Prospect Hill!

Bimala learned how to cook from her mother and by taking a cooking class in high school. "We make certain dishes for important cultural festivals," she says. "Like for Dishain [a 10-day festival in the fall honoring the goddess Durga], when we have goat meat, beaten rice and cucumber pickle. You need to know how to cook these dishes, so we pass these recipes on from one generation to the next."

Bimala's daughter Sabrina says that if you're Nepalese and female, learning how to cook comes automatically. "You don't have a choice," she says with a smile. "It's just part of growing up."

The achar (or tomato pickle) recipe here features timur, an exotic spice that has a fragrant, citric aroma and numbs the tongue slightly—especially if eaten on its own. The achar can be served as an appetizer with chapati bread or as an accompaniment to a meal. It makes a lovely, piquant complement to kidney bean curry and pulao. "My daughter makes tomato pickle with timur very well," says Bimala. "I like to tease her that she is an achar specialist. Pulao, a flavorful rice, is usually made for special occasions in Nepal—it's always served at weddings, for example. Yet it also goes nicely with these two dishes."

"You can't have a meal without rice," Sabrina chimes in. "All Nepalis are addicted to rice!"

Recipes: Bimala Thapa | Text, Recipe Testing & Food Styling: Rachel Strutt | Photography: Dustin Kerstein (unless otherwise noted)

### PULAO Serves 4
# (NEPALI RICE WITH NUTS AND CARDAMOM)

## Ingredients

1½ cups basmati rice*
1½ tablespoons butter
¼ cup cashews

¼ cup golden raisins
1 black cardamom pods*
3 green cardamom pods*

## Directions

1. Rinse rice, then soak for a few minutes.
2. Melt butter and sauté cashews over medium heat for a few minutes until they are browned; then add golden raisins and cardamom.
3. If using a rice cooker, add rice, nut and spice mixture and appropriate amount of water. If using a pan, add rice to nut and spice mixture and cover with ½ inch of water; cook for the amount of time given on the rice cooking directions—about 15 minutes.

## GOLBHEDA KO ACHAR WITH TIMUR AND DHANIYA (TOMATO TIMUR PICKLE)

## Ingredients

3 plum tomatoes
1 green chili pepper (jalepeño or other)
½ teaspoon of red chili powder
   (or to taste)
1 clove garlic (no more than a teaspoon)
4-5 timur cloves*, crushed with a
   mortar and pestle

⅓ cup fresh cilantro
   (plus a little extra for final step)
1 tablespoon of oil (mustard oil*
   is preferable), plus a little
   more for frying tomatoes

## Directions

1. Cut the three tomatoes in half and place flat side down in a small amount of oil in a frying pan over medium-high heat (or on a grill, for added flavor). Fry or grill both sides of the tomato about two minutes each.
2. When tomatoes are half cooked, put them in a food processor with all the other ingredients and purée.
3. Put in a small bowl and sprinkle a little more cilantro on top. Serve with chapati bread as an appetizer or with pulao and rajma for a delicious Nepali meal.

Sacks of rice at New Bombay Market.

## RAJMA (NEPALI KIDNEY BEAN CURRY) Serves 4

### Ingredients

1 teaspoon ground turmeric*

1 tomato, chopped

1 onion, chopped

2 tablespoons vegetable oil

1 teaspoon grated or minced ginger

1 teaspoon garlic

1 teaspoon meat masala powder or ground cumin*

¼ teaspoon red chili powder (or to taste)*

1 teaspoon salt (or to taste)

1 can (13 ounces) of kidney beans, washed and drained

⅓ cup fresh chopped cilantro

### Directions

1. Brown the chopped onion in oil for about 5 minutes on medium heat.

2. Add tumeric and stir. Then add tomato, masala powder or cumin, chili powder, salt, ginger and garlic; mix and heat through for a few minutes while rinsing the kidney beans.

3. Add kidney beans and cook for 5-7 minutes. Add about ½ cup water (more or less depending on how you like the consistency).

4. Serve with chopped cilantro on top.

Clockwise, from top left: precooked ingredients for the okra etouffée; jalapeño, which adds a kick to the etouffée; a trifecta of Haitian cuisine: etouffée (on green plate), riz au djon djon (on yellow plate) and fried plantains.

# OKRA ETOUFFÉE, RIZ AU DJON DJON & FRIED PLANTAINS

**A Port-au-Prince native shares three recipes for a Haitian meal as exotic and colorful as the island nation itself.**

Julia Fairclough (left) and Judith Laguerre cook a Haitian meal together.

Judith Laguerre's family can always tell when she is starting to make one of her complex, colorful and labor-intensive Haitian meals. It's not the savory smell that gives this talented cook away, but the sound of pounding and scratching as Judith uses her *pilon*—a mortar and pestle to grind herbs.

Judith takes pride in making all of her meals from scratch and abstains from using fancy electric devices to grind and chop. "Sometimes I think I should change my way of cooking," she says. "But I just can't do it. We cook as we did in Haiti—everything takes time."

Before she gets busy in the kitchen, Judith heads to the shops, including La Internacional in Union Square, where she is able to pick up essential Haitian ingredients like chayote, malanga, farine de banane (banana flour) and hard-to-find djon djon mushrooms. "In Haiti, djon djon mushrooms are quite a delicacy," Judith says. "Often when people come back from visiting Haiti, they bring back some dried djon djons in their suitcase."

The rich amalgamation of flavors in Haitian cuisine speaks to the country's turbulent history, which has shaped Kreyol cooking—a mixture of French, African, Spanish and indigenous cuisines. Certain ingredients, Judith explains, are staples in nearly every Haitian dish: onion, garlic, thyme, cloves, black pepper, hot pepper and parsley.

She adds, however, that the main ingredients in Haitian dishes are patience and an eye for color. One of her salads, for example, will contain a rainbow of blanched carrots, beets, broccoli, red peppers and white potatoes. "Color is very important in Haitian cuisine," Judith says. "We want our food to look as good as it tastes."

Recipes & Food Styling: **Judith Laguerre** | Text & Recipe Testing: **Julia Fairclough** | Photography: **Dustin Kerstein**

## OKRA ETOUFFÉE   Serves 4

### Ingredients

1 pound thinly sliced beef
1 tablespoon lime juice
½ teaspoon white or red vinegar
½ jalapeño pepper chopped
½ red bell pepper, chopped
½ green bell pepper, chopped
1 large onion, chopped
5 cloves garlic, crushed

2 scallions, chopped
¼ cup chopped tomato, drained
1 tablespoon each fresh thyme
   and parsley, chopped
½ teaspoon crushed cloves
2 tablespoons olive oil
1 tablespoon tomato paste
3 cups fresh or frozen okra

### Directions

1. Cover the beef in a marinade combining all the other ingredients except the okra, olive oil and tomato paste; also reserve half of the onion and red and green pepper to use later. Marinate for a half hour.
2. Cook marinated beef with its liquid, plus 1 cup warm water over low heat, until water is completely evaporated.
3. Add the meat and brown slowly by

stirring frequently; while stirring, add a few tablespoons of warm water.
4. Add tomato paste; stir until dissolved.
5. Add okra and stir to mix. Taste and adjust the seasoning, if necessary.
6. Add ½ cup warm water, and remaining onion and green and red pepper.
7. Cover and simmer for a half hour.

## FRIED PLANTAINS   Serves 4-6

### Ingredients

3 plantains
vegetable oil for frying

### Directions

1. Peel plantains and cut each one diagonally into 5 pieces.
2. Soak in salt water for three minutes.
3. Dry each side and press flat.
4. Heat ½ inch oil in a frying pan over medium heat; fry plantains for 2 minutes each side.
5. Briefly soak plantain pieces in the salt water and refry for 1 or 2 minutes each side, until golden and crispy.

# RIZ AU DJON-DJON Serves 4

## Ingredients

½ cup djon djon mushrooms•
3 tablespoons olive oil
5 cloves garlic, crushed
2 scallions, chopped
1 cup fresh or frozen peas

salt and black pepper
½ bunch parsley and ½ bunch thyme, tied
together in a bouquet
1 cup long white rice
½ teaspoon crushed cloves

*Shopping tip: Find djon djon mushrooms at La Internacional; they are sold in small plastic bags. If you have trouble finding them, ask the friendly owners for help.

## Directions

1. Boil 2 cups of hot water, remove from stove. Soak djon djons mushrooms in this water for 10 minutes.
2. Drain the mushrooms by pushing through a cheesecloth or fine sieve. Discard the mushrooms and keep the djon djon broth.
3. Add olive oil to a hot pot. Add crushed garlic and scallions, stirring frequently until golden.
4. Add the peas, salt and pepper; stir for one minute.

5. Add the 2 cups of djon djon broth and bouquet of parsley and thyme. Bring to a boil.
6. Add rice and cloves; stir to mix.
7. Taste and adjust the seasoning with salt and pepper, if necessary.
8. Cook on high heat for 5 minutes and then on very low heat for 25 minutes. Rice should come out very light and fluffy.

# TIELLA DI GAETA

**Mayor Curtatone and his mom spend an afternoon making a centuries-old Italian dish.**

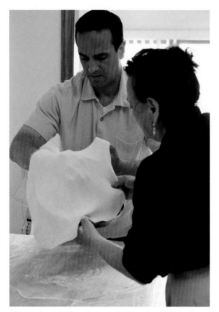

Mayor Joseph Curtatone and his mother, Maria, line a pan with crust for tiella di Gaeta.

Just outside Union Square, on a gentle slope of Prospect Hill, the Italians are cooking. There's Maria, a proud grandmother and force of nature, and her grown son, Giuseppe, who handles a thin disk of rolled-out dough, carefully laying it on top of a round pan. Once the pan has been filled with a shiny spinach mixture, he crimps the overlapping edges with a fork and his fingers. "Like this, Ma?" he asks. She corrects him with loving authority. "No, no," she says, and then shows him how to do it the right way. The traditional way. This is an important lesson for Giuseppe, the man we know as Somerville Mayor Joseph Curtatone.

Maria's hands are always moving: mixing, kneading, gesturing. Like many Italian grandmothers, she cooks a lot, for family and other seniors who can no longer cook for themselves. "I like cooking!" she exclaims. "I like work!" For Joe, it's a chance to commit to memory a recipe whose exact measurements are hard to capture. Everything is measured by hand or by eye. A palmful of salt. A swoosh of oil. A few shakes of hot pepper.

Tiella is a centuries-old rustic dish from the seaside town of Gaeta. It dates back to the 1800s, when the wives of fishermen baked up these savory pies to put in their husbands' lunch baskets. Today in Gaeta, tiella is an Easter favorite and a highlight at outdoor festivals. Gaeta, about 60 miles north of Naples, is a sister city of Somerville and the birthplace of Maria and her late husband, Cosmo.

Tiella consists of two thin layers of dough crimped around various fillings: spinach, octopus, and escarole and baccalà (salted cod), among others. "In the old days, people used whatever they had in the garden or brought home from the sea," Joe explains. Today, it's not so different. Both Maria and Joe gather their ingredients at the local farmers' market and the nearby Market Basket in Union Square. Maria's first choice, though, is picking vegetables from her own garden.

Recipes: Maria Curtatone | Text: Susan Abbattista | Photography: Rachel Blumenthal | Recipe Testing: Catherine Aiello

Maria Curtatone's hands are always moving: mixing, kneading, gesturing.

## TIELLA DI GAETA
Each tiella serves 4–6 (main course) or 8–10 (appetizer)

## DOUGH

To follow Maria's dough recipe, go to the recipe section of Nibble (www.somervilleartscouncil.org/nibble). Maria also says you can use ready-made pizza dough, available at supermarkets or some local pizzerias.

## SPINACH FILLING

### Ingredients

2 bags (2 pounds) fresh, whole spinach leaves (washed and drained)

3 cloves garlic (finely minced or crushed)

⅓ cup whole Gaeta olives, pitted and halved*

⅓ cup olive oil, plus 1 tablespoon for brushing top (or use corn oil, like Maria)

salt (to taste)

red pepper flakes (to taste)

### Directions

1. Wash spinach leaves in cold water, removing all grit. Let drain.
2. In a large bowl, combine spinach with garlic.
3. Mix in ⅓ cup oil and pitted olives.
4. Add salt and red pepper to taste.
5. Mix spinach filling with clean hands or a wooden spoon.

# ONION AND TOMATO FILLING

## Ingredients

2 pounds yellow onions, thinly sliced
⅓ cup olive (or corn) oil,
  plus 1 tablespoon for brushing top
6 ounces crushed tomatoes
½ cup chopped fresh parsley
salt (to taste)
red pepper flakes (to taste)

## Directions

1. Put sliced onions in a large bowl, and add ⅓ cup oil and 1 tablespoon of salt (or to taste).
2. Mix and allow to sit for at least an hour, or until onions become soft.
3. Add crushed tomatoes, parsley, and 1 tablespoon red pepper flakes (or to taste). Mix well.

# TIELLA ASSEMBLY

## Directions

1. Place oven racks in the low and middle positions; preheat oven to 400°F.
2. Have ready a 10- to 12-inch round cake pan with 2-inch sides. Oil the pan with olive oil, even if it is nonstick.
3. If not using premade dough, prepare the dough.
4. While the dough is rising, prepare the spinach or onion and tomato filling.
5. Punch down the dough and turn it out onto a lightly floured work surface.
6. Divide the dough into 2 pieces, one slightly larger than the other. Using a rolling pin or your fingers, stretch and press the larger piece into a round about 16 inches in diameter and 1/16 inch thick.
7. Transfer the round to the pan and press it into the bottom and up the sides, leaving at least a 1- to 2-inch overhang. Fill with the spinach or onion mixture, spreading evenly.

*Shopping tip:These ingredients are available at Capone Foods and other Italian markets.

8. Roll out the remaining dough into a 12-inch round about 1/16 inch thick. Carefully lay it over the filling and trim to size with no overhang. Bring the overhang of the lower crust up over the edges of the top crust and press against the top. Crimp the edges together, forming a wavy edge.
9. Prick the top in several places with a fork and brush lightly with oil. Bake on lowest rack until top begins to turn a light golden brown, about 30–40 minutes. Move to middle rack and cook until firm, about 20 more minutes.
10. Transfer to a wire rack and let cool. Serve the tart at room temperature, sliced in wedges.

# SPICY COCONUT CURRIED GOAT STEW

**Our Parisian intern Vera chats with the folks at Highland Kitchen—where you'll find this tasty stew—and WellFoods Plus, the place to get your goat.**

WellFoods Plus sells freshly butchered goat meat.

Perhaps you already eat goat meat. Or maybe you are considering taking the plunge. Either way, you will be in good company: according to a recent article in the *New York Times*, goat is the most consumed meat in the world.

This recipe comes from Mark Romano, head chef at Highland Kitchen, one of the 'ville's most popular eateries. Before coming to Somerville, Romano was chef at Green Street Grill in Cambridge, where he inherited this Caribbean stew recipe from that restaurant's former chef John Levins. Since then, Romano has tweaked things a bit and developed an off-the-bone version. It is now one of Highland Kitchen's trademark dishes!

Romano uses goat imported from New Zealand or Australia, but you don't have to go that far to get your goat. Just head to WellFoods Plus, the Halal market in Union Square. Halal means "permitted" or "lawful" in Arabic, and when referring to meat, it signifies that the animal has been blessed by an imam and slaughtered in accordance with Islamic law. Jahinger Kabir, who owns WellFoods Plus with his wife, Rokeya, tells us that some farms simply play a recorded blessing before slaughtering goats, but theirs come from a farm in western Massachusetts where an actual imam blesses the goats.

Rokeya reports that WellFoods Plus sells between 25 to 30 goats per week. Haitians are big goat meat customers, along with Indians, Pakistanis and Nepalis. Goat is an especially popular dish during Ramadan and the Nepali holiday Dasara. During holiday seasons, WellFoods Plus sells around 50 goats per week—and many families order goat meat far in advance.

Rokeya says goat meat is tastier and healthier than beef; it is leaner and contains less cholesterol. When stopping for ingredients to make Highland Kitchen's spicy stew, Rokeya recommends buying leg meat, which is the most tender.

Recipe: Highland Kitchen, adapted by Genevieve Rajewski & Ryan Redmond | Text: Vera Vidal
Photography: Dustin Kerstein (unless otherwise noted) | Recipe Testing: Ryan Redmond

# GOAT STEW Serves 4

## Ingredients

2 tablespoons olive oil
5 pounds bone-in goat meat
1 medium Spanish onion, sliced
2 carrots, cut into 1-inch pieces
1 clove garlic, finely chopped
½ Scotch bonnet or other hot pepper,
   seeded and finely chopped (if you like it
   hot, add up until 3)
1 piece (1 inch) fresh ginger, finely chopped
1 tablespoon chopped fresh thyme

1½ cups white wine
4 cups chicken stock
4 ounces calabaza* (or butternut squash), cut into 2-inch pieces
4 ounces chayote* (or summer squash), cut into 2-inch pieces
4 ounces malanga* (or sweet potato), cut into 2-inch pieces
2 cans (12 ounces each) coconut milk
2 tablespoons curry powder
1 tablespoon ground allspice
salt and pepper, to taste
2 cups canned whole tomatoes, crushed

## Directions

1. Set the oven at 400°F.
2. In a large flameproof casserole over high heat, heat the oil. Add half the meat and let it brown, without moving, for 3 minutes. Turn and brown the other side. Remove from pan and brown the remaining meat in the same way. Remove all the meat from the pan.
3. Add the onion and carrots to the pan. Cook, stirring often, for 5 minutes. Add the garlic, chili pepper, ginger, thyme, curry powder, allspice, salt and pepper. Cook, stirring, for 3 minutes or until the spices are aromatic. Stir in the tomatoes, wine and stock. Return the meat to the pan. Bring to a boil, cover the pan, and place in the oven. Cook for 2 to 2½ hours or until the meat falls off the bone.
4. With a slotted spoon remove the meat from the pan; set aside. Add calabaza, chayote, malanga, and coconut milk to the pan. Simmer for 20 minutes or until all the vegetables are tender.
5. Remove the meat from the bones in large chunks. Return the meat to the stew. Bring to a boil, taste for seasoning, and add more salt and pepper, if you like.
6. Serve with jasmine rice.

> *Shopping Tip: Find all spices at Indian markets, except allspice berries, which you'll find at La Internacional and most Caribbean markets. Find calabaza, chayote and malanga at Market Basket.

# CURRY POWDER

## Ingredients

1 tablespoon coriander seeds*
1 tablespoon cumin seeds*
1 tablespoon black mustard seeds*
1 tablespoon fennel seeds*
½ tablespoon fenugreek seeds*
½ tablespoon allspice berries*
½ teaspoon cloves
2½ tablespoons ground turmeric*

## Directions

1. Toast the whole spices in a heavy pan (such as cast-iron) over medium-low heat. Give them a shake or stir from time to time.
2. When you begin to smell the aroma of the spices, add the turmeric, give the spices a stir, and after 30 seconds turn off the heat. Pour the spices onto a plate and allow them to cool. The whole process may take two or three minutes. Pay close attention not to burn the spices.
3. Once cool, grind the mix in a spice grinder.

Clockwise from top left: Union Square's farmers' market; Catherine Aiello's illustration of Sherman Market; Lourdes Smith of Fiore di Nonno "paddling" a batch of burrata; a bench outside Sherman Cafe; tomatoes at the Union Square Farmers' Market; Elaine Hsieh and Catharine Sweeney of EH Chocolatier.

# Locavore & Healthy Fare

Rachel Strutt

 HOME GROWN

 SPRING GARDEN SALAD, WONTONS WITH CHILI DIPPING SAUCE

 FARMER CHEESE AND RED PEPPER SALAD WITH TOASTED PINENUTS

 NORTH INDIAN DAL & ROTI

I ♥ MY FARMER
the farms and flavors of Rhode Island and Massachusetts at FarmFresh.org

PrintBrigade.com

Rachel Strutt

# HOME GROWN

**Locally grown and produced food cultivates a sense of community in Union Square.**

Text by Genevieve Rajewski | Illustrations by Catherine Aiello

On this particuluar morning, the scene is tranquil at Journeyman—Union Square's 30-seat restaurant dedicated to craft preparations using local ingredients. Co-owners Meg Grady-Troia, Diana Kudajarova and Tse Wei Lim relax over a pot of strong coffee and freshly baked bread with butter and jam. Kudajarova's and Lim's mixed-breed dog, Gnocchi, sniffs around underfoot, scouring the floor for any getaway crumbs.

The relaxed vibe won't last for long. Soon, Grady-Troia, the restaurant's general manager, will start preparing copious notes on tonight's tasting menus for the incoming servers. Chef Kudajarova will head into the kitchen to begin prepping plates for the three-, five- and seven-course meals. And chef Lim will hit the road to pick up four lambs from the Blood Farm slaughterhouse in Groton, Massachusetts.

Although Journeyman's staff works hard to serve up local food in season, the restaurant's proprietors wouldn't consider running their business any other way. It's a sentiment shared by a surprising number of establishments and organizations in Union Square, which together make the neighborhood a mecca for in-season and locally grown foods.

There's nowhere else around Boston where you will find such a treasure trove of local eating: a Saturday farmers' market; a new Thursday evening farmers' market called "Swirl and Slice"; Sherman Market, which offers one-stop shopping for locally produced meats, veggies, fruit, tofu, cheeses, grains and prepared foods seven days a week; and WellFoods Plus, a tiny halal food market that does a big business in local meat. Meanwhile, cheeses by Fiore de Nonno and chocolates by Taza and EH Chocolatier are all produced just a few blocks away. These businesses can survive in such close proximity—and actually thrive—because they have built a community that complements, rather than competes with, each other.

The locavore organization with the oldest roots in Union Square is the Somerville Community Growing Center. According to Lisa Brukalacchio, a Friends of the Community Growing Center board member, the community garden was founded in 1993 to serve as a demonstration site for urban agriculture and a place where high school and elementary students could learn about science and nutrition in a hands-on way.

True to the spirit of eating local, the center also had a mission to cultivate community. "Around the time we started looking for funding to create the center, a study came out showing that gardening was the number-one recreational activity in the country," says Brukalacchio, who is a co-founder of the community garden just outside Union Square. "Other city parks support soccer or softball. We argued that this could be public space that helps people in a city environment understand that they too can participate in gardening."

Their efforts paid off in ways that Brukalacchio could not have predicted. "Kids somehow know what to do when there's a plant that gives juicy fruit. Put kids near a blackberry bush and they just go for it," she says. "But in teaching the kids, we found an unexpected avenue for connecting with their parents."

This was particularly true for residents who were not just new to Union Square, but also to the United States. Brukalacchio says that recent immigrants find comfort when they spot fruits and vegetables from their homeland growing here in Somerville. She cites as one example a woman from Puerto Rico who was surprised to see familiar peppers growing at the center when she came to pick up her 4-year-old son from a gardening class. Brukalacchio introduced the woman to Somerville's community garden network, and soon the whole family was farming together in Union Square.

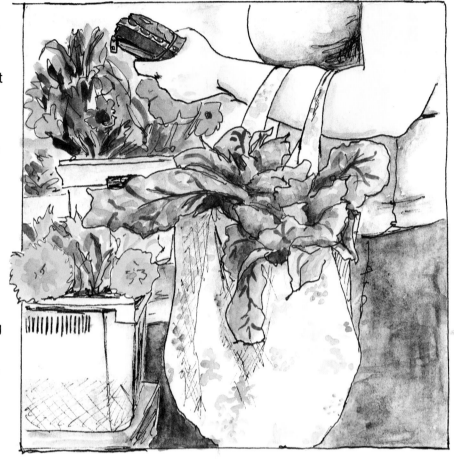

"They found something do together as a family," Brukalacchio says. "And by growing food they were familiar with from their homeland, they both kept a link to their country of origin and rooted themselves in the earth here."

Today, the Community Growing Center hosts local-food-oriented festivities year-round: a seed and plant exchange in spring; summer gardening classes food film screenings; grape and apple pressing using the garden's harvest in fall; and a maple syrup boil-down each March.

The center also partners with Groundwork Somerville to sell its products at the Union Square Farmers' Market. At their booth, you will find Swiss chard, kale, cucumbers, grape leaves and kohlrabi grown right outside the square—as well as herbal teas and maple syrup made from Somerville sources.

The Union Square Farmers' Market also has strengthened the local-food movement far beyond city limits.

"Our farmers say that Union Square is their most profitable farmers' market—more so even than Copley Square, Government Center and Lexington, and that the people who come really know their food," says Mimi Graney, executive director of Union Square Main Streets, which produces the market together with the City of Somerville. "They say that the customers are friendly, very knowledgeable about ingredients and more open to experimenting with new foods. That has influenced our farmers, who are willing to grow more unusual products because they know people in Somerville will buy them."

Attendance at the farmers' market—which runs on Saturdays from 9am to 1pm, June through November—has doubled over the past three years. About 2,000 people visit the market on Union Square Plaza every weekend. "Attendees really reflect the international character of the neighborhood, and you see that reflected in what's for sale," says Graney. She notes, for example, that Flats Mentor Farm sells produce like baby bok choy, Thai basil, misuna, pea tendrils, pumpkin vines, lemon grass and other ingredients used by local Asian cooks.

The strong demand for local products allowed the market to grow to 20 vendors in 2011—adding a cheese vendor, two wineries, a hummus maker, a nut vendor and a fish merchant.

"The Union Square Farmers' Market is well organized and brings in really good products," notes personal chef J.J. Gonson, one of the region's best known and most passionate advocates of local food. "It also is very forward-thinking compared with a lot of other farmers' markets. They have embraced supporting prepared foods and value-added items—which are really important to farmers' profitability because they can be made in the summer and canned and sold through the year."

The market's festival atmosphere also sets it apart from many in the Boston area. Visitors can count on finding a different band performing every week, activities for kids and special events like canning workshops.

"It's like a block party every week," says Graney, who notes that the plaza did not always feel like such a vibrant place. "The market was created [in 2005] with the purpose of animating the plaza. People forget that Union Square used to shut down on the weekends. It was dead. Now it's super busy, and people really identify the plaza with the farmers' market. Food brings people together."

Noting the area's ravenous appetite for local fare, in spring of

2012 Union Square Main Streets launched a *second* weekly food market. Thursday nights from mid June through mid September, the Swirl & Slice market features locally made wine, cheese, jams, pickles and specialty products like cured meats and cut flowers. Music and food-themed activities, including the Arts Council's international market tours, take place in conjunction with the market.

The success of the Union Square Farmers' Market inspired Karyn Coughlin and her husband, Ben Dryer, to open Sherman Market in 2009. The couple had been operating their popular Sherman Café for six years when they learned that retail space next door had become available.

"Right from the start, we tried to get produce from local vendors for the café because we liked the idea of keeping the money in our local economy," says Coughlin. "And with the farmers' market taking off the way it did, we thought there was probably a demand for year-round and week-round availability of local foods."

The market sells Fiore di Nonno cheeses and Taza Chocolate—both produced a few blocks away—and occasionally offers produce that was grown by students at schools citywide through Groundwork Somerville's gardening education program. The market also works directly with Vermont and Massachusetts farms that deliver via Metro Pedal Power's Farmers to You cargo-bike delivery service and with Ocean State producers via the nonprofit Farm Fresh Rhode Island program.

Interestingly, the fresh produce has not sold as well as Sherman Market's owners had expected. "It turns out that people love to go to the farmers' market—which is awesome," explains Coughlin. "So we've scaled that back so we're now just filling in the gaps between Saturdays."

However, Sherman Market has seen a stronger-than-anticipated demand for meat, as well as its own line of prepared foods made with local ingredients. "The stuff we make ourselves is very popular, so we plan on doing more with prepared foods," says Coughlin. "Right now, we offer house-made hummus, cream cheeses, soups and stocks, salad specials and ice cream sandwiches featuring Maple's ice cream in our cookies."

Gonson notes that eating local by shopping at stores like Sherman Market can bolster a sense of community. "It fosters good will," she explains. "You and your neighborhood business owners get to know each other. And that's how you can together create a healthy, vibrant community. It's better for quality of life all around."

—*Genevieve Rajewski writes about food, animal issues and much more for publications such as* Edible Boston *and the* Boston Globe. *Read more at www.genevieverajewski.com.* ●

# SPRING GARDEN SALAD & WONTONS WITH CHILI DIPPING SAUCE

**A Tufts student cooks with a Shanghai native and learns how the Chinese celebrate a new season.**

Anna Larson Williams with Zhongshun Zhou (center) and Rongwen Zhang.

Rongwen Zhang, a Shanghai native currently living in Union Square with her husband, Zhongshun Zhou, was eager to share this meal—traditional Chinese cuisine that has been perfected through the generations. The cool and fresh salad is the perfect match for the wontons drizzled with fiery dipping sauce.

Rongwen says that everyone in China knows how to cook what she calls the Spring Garden Salad. She associates this salad with spring because of its colors, which include shades of green punctuated with the orange of the carrots. Rongwen declares that this salad is a harbinger of the season: "When eating it, you feel that spring is coming early!"

The salad also incites better moods and warmer feelings through its nutritional value. Rongwen, who has a background in chemical engineering and is well versed in nutrition, tells us that cabbage—a key ingredient in the salad—is loaded with vitamin C and a few different B vitamins. Rongwen also explains that cellophane noodles, made with mung bean flour, encourage weight loss because, although high in carbohydrates, they are low in fat.

Another advance signal of spring is Chinese New Year. Known in China as Spring Festival, it marks the Lunar New Year and falls in late January or February. Many Chinese eat wontons when they celebrate this holiday, so wontons have come to represent a time when families come together and appreciate what life brings. Rongwen adds that wontons are served at nearly every party. These delicious dumplings are traditionally made with pork, but we also offer a vegetarian version as a healthy alternative. A word of caution: Rongwen's chili pepper sauce has a serious kick. Brace yourself!

Recipe: Rongwen Zhang | Text: Anna Larson Williams | Photography: Dustin Kerstein | Recipe Testing: Anna Larson Williams and Julie Betters

**Recipe tip**: Make the chili sauce first; it lasts up to 3 days.

**\*Shopping tip**: Find dried chili peppers at New Bombay; find other ingredients at Reliable Market and other Asian grocery stores.

# CHILI SAUCE

## Ingredients

½ cup canola oil

20-25 dried red chili peppers*, chopped

3 cloves garlic, chopped

3 tablespoons peeled and finely chopped ginger

1 tablespoon soy sauce (or more to taste)

¼ teaspoon sugar

½ teaspoon salt

2 teaspoons rice vinegar*

## Directions

1. Heat oil in a small pan on medium heat. When hot, add dried red chili peppers, (seeds and shell included), garlic and ginger.

2. Turn off heat immediately and stir in one direction. Pour into a glass bowl (or another nonreactive type bowl); set aside until mixture reaches room temperature.

3. Add soy sauce to taste (at least 1 tablespoon), sugar, salt, and vinegar. In a blender or food processor blend the sauce until the peppers are small but still chunky. Set aside, or cover and refrigerate until ready.

# CHINESE SPRING GARDEN SALAD Serves 4

## Ingredients

1 teaspoon sugar

3 tablespoons rice vinegar*

1 teaspoon salt

1 package green bean noodles* (we recommend Longkou vermicelli; packaging includes bright pink netting)

½ head napa cabbage*, thinly sliced, rinsed, patted dry

2 medium carrots, grated on the large side of a grater

cilantro (basil can be substituted if you prefer)

## Directions

1. Mix the salt, vinegar, and sugar. Cover and put it in the refrigerator for 2-3 days (or, follow quick version: put mixture in the microwave for 5-10 seconds, stir and refrigerate until cooled).

2. Boil water in a large pot; add 3-4 bundles of the green bean noodles (they come in bundles inside the package). Leave in for 1-2 minutes, gently stirring. Remove the noodles from heat once they soften.

3. Strain the noodles and place immediately in a bowl of cold water. This will prevent the noodles from sticking to each other. Set aside.

4. In a large bowl add the cabbage, grated carrot, cilantro and cooled noodles.

5. Add the desired amount of previously made chili sauce to the cooled salt, vinegar, sugar mixture. Stir together and add to the noodles, mixing well (mixing with your hands works best).

# CHINESE WONTONS (VEGETARIAN AND PORK OPTIONS)

## Ingredients

1 package wonton or gyoza wrappers*
2 cups napa cabbage*, thinly sliced, rinsed and patted dry
½ cup chopped green beans
½ cup chopped celery (1 stalk)
2 tablespoons canola oil
4 scallions, chopped
1 tablespoon rice vinegar*

1½ teaspoons peeled and finely chopped ginger
1 tablespoon soy sauce*
¼ teaspoon sugar
¼ teaspoon salt
1 egg white
2 teaspoons sesame oil*
optional: ½ pound ground pork

## Directions for filling

1. In a pan with enough water to cover the bottom, add the cabbage, green beans and celery. Cover and put on medium heat. Steam vegetables for 15 minutes, or until they are soft.
2. Strain vegetables and pat with a paper towel to soak up excess water.
3. Add to a bowl with remaining ingredients. Stir.
4. If you'd like traditional wontons, add ground pork to the mixture (this will make filling for more than 20).

## Directions for wontons

1. To assemble wontons, spoon 1 heaping teaspoon of the filling into the center of the wrapper.
2. If using sqiare wonton wrappers, wet all four edges, bring all four corners to the middle and press together to make a purse. The bottom will be flat. If using round gyoza wrappers, wet edges and fold in half; press edges together to make a half circle (photos feature wontons made with round gyoza wrappers.)
3. Put wontons on a cookie sheet and freeze for 1 hour.
4. Take small batches of the frozen wontons and steam over boiling water in a metal steamer for 15 minutes.
5. Heat a pan with canola oil over medium heat; when hot, add wontons in batches and pan-fry until the bottoms are golden brown, about 5 minutes.
6. Serve with chili sauce for dipping.

Use either square wonton wrappers to make purse-shaped wontons or use circular gyoza wrappers (as seen in these photos) to make crescent-shaped wontons.

# FARMER CHEESE AND RED PEPPER SALAD WITH TOASTED PINENUTS

**Artist and Somerville Arts Council board member Alexis Kochka follows in the footsteps of her locavore grandmother.**

The Union Square Farmers' Market; a selection of locally produced milk at Sherman Market.

Every culture has a variation on farmer cheese: Indian paneer and Mexican queso fresco are just two examples. It's the workingman's cheese. But don't be fooled—it is also delicious and easy to make.

I adapted this recipe from one I found in a yellowed copy of the 1972 *New York Times Natural Foods Cookbook* that I inherited from my grandmother. From the pages of this cookbook, with its healthy hippie slant, my grandmother tirelessly created feasts for her family of 7 children—the youngest two being twins!

"Locavore" may be a relatively new word, but the concept, of course, is an old one. My grandmother grew veggies and shopped locally long before it was trendy. I have a feeling she would have loved living in Somerville, especially Union Square—with its bustling farmers' market and small mom-and-pop stores.

I didn't have to go far for this recipe's ingredients. I took a jaunt over Prospect Hill and landed at Sherman Market for some frosty white milk in a clear glass bottle from Thatcher Farm. Next, I hit up the Union Square Farmers' Market for red peppers and fresh herbs. After concocting the salad at home, my husband and I dug in. Delicious. I think my grandmother would have concurred.

Recipe, Text & Food Styling: **Alexis Kochka** | Photography: **Rachel Strutt** (this page), **Alexis Kochka** (next page)
Recipe Testing: **Christine McLellan, Ellen Kramer** and **Leah Gourley Lindsay**

# FARMER CHEESE AND RED PEPPER SALAD WITH TOASTED PINE NUTS

## CHEESE

### Ingredients

1 gallon whole milk*
8 tablespoons lemon juice
cheesecloth

### Directions

Make the cheese the night before, or 2 hours before you plan to serve this salad.

1. Pour a gallon of milk into a large stockpot. Over medium heat, bring the milk to a rolling boil; stir regularly to keep from burning.
2. Stir in the lemon juice while the milk is boiling; then remove milk from the burner. You'll see that the milk curdles from the lemon; these curds will form the cheese.
3. Double-line a strainer with cheesecloth. Make sure you have enough cheesecloth so that you can wrap the curds in the strainer. Pour the curds and whey into the strainer. The curds will be caught in the cheesecloth, and the whey will pass through.
4. Carefully use the sides of the cloth to bundle up the curds and wring out the excess liquid. The curds will be very hot, so be careful.
5. Once the whey has drained, push the curds together to form a cheese ball. Then place the cloth-wrapped curd bundle on a cutting board. Balance another cutting board or a heavy plate on the flattened bundle. On top of the plate or board place a pot of water to press even more whey out.
6. Let cheese set for 2 hours without refrigerating. Don't let it sit much longer or the cheese will be too dry. The final consistency should be like feta cheese or tofu.

*Shopping tip: Find local milk at Sherman Market or other locavore-friendly markets; find produce at the Union Square Farmers' Market or your local farmers' market!

## SALAD   Serves 4

### Ingredients

4 red peppers
½ cup olive oil
4 cloves of garlic
1 bunch of fresh basil, chopped coarsely
8 sprigs of oregano
⅛ cup balsamic vinegar
¼ cup toasted pine nuts
½ cup black olives, chopped
kosher salt, to taste
black pepper, to taste
optional: 1 cup white beans or 1 cup farro

### Directions

For roasting the peppers:
1. Wash and dry peppers.
2. Char peppers on a grill, turning with tongs. If you have a gas oven, you can also char peppers directly over a flame, using tongs. Or, broil peppers in the oven, leaving door slightly open and turning when necessary. Once the pepper is partially blackened and looks deflated, it is done.
3. Place peppers in a brown paper bag and fold to seal; or wrap them in aluminum foil. Leave for 10-15 minutes.
4. Remove peppers; using a knife, cut off blackened skin.
5. Cut peppers into 1-inch pieces.

For salad:
1. Slice the cheese into 1-inch cubes.
2. Oil a nonstick pan with ½ cup olive oil, or enough to thoroughly coat the pan.
3. Slice 2 cloves of garlic and sauté over medium heat until translucent.
4. Add the cheese cubes to the oil and sauté until the edges turn golden brown.
5. If you like, add white beans and heat through.
6. Add salt and pepper to taste.
7. Remove from heat.
8. In a bowl combine the cheese, red peppers, black olives, farro (if using), basil and oregano and drizzle with olive oil and balsamic vinegar; top with toasted pine nuts. Serve at room temperature or chilled.

# NORTH INDIAN DAL AND ROTI

**Looking to increase your iron, fiber and protein consumption? A Shape Up Somerville scribe suggests a culinary jaunt to northern India!**

Jill Sahil's husband, Shanker, presents his dal and roti.

My husband's family grew up in northeast India in the ancient city of Arrah, where many families are vegetarian and dal and roti are staples. Dal is like a thick lentil soup spiced up with coriander, chili, curry powder and cumin; roti is a traditional Indian flat bread made with wheat flour and typically used to scoop up the dal. When I ask my husband, Shanker, about memories associated with these dishes, he replies simply, "Dal and roti was a meal that we would have when my mother needed to go shopping and there was not much left in the house!"

Growing up in Montana, my family ate a lot of processed and ready-made foods. Now, as an adult who is starting my own family, I love cooking healthy, fresh, whole foods. I've often noted how my husband's cooking is inherently healthy. Whereas we Americans might take vitamins or eat products enhanced with vitamin D or iron, the dishes of northeast India are already nutrient rich. For example, dal is made with orange lentils, which are high in iron and fiber; roti is made with wheat flour, which is high in protein.

We cook dal and roti weekly not only because it's healthy—it's also delicious! Plus, these dishes will fill your house with a warm and inviting scent as the roasted spices linger in the air. Dal is simple to prepare, but as with so many Indian dishes, there are a slew of spices involved. We find these spices at great prices at Little India in Union Square, where store owner Dipti Umesh greets us with a friendly smile. My husband says the selection of unique foods and spices at Little India reminds him of the markets he visited as a child.

This recipe for dal and roti has been in my husband's family for generations. We are thrilled to share it with the community and can't wait for you to experience a little bit of northeast India in your kitchen.

Recipe: Shanker Sahil | Text: Jill Sahil | Photography: Somerby Jones | Recipe Testing: Christine McLellan

## NORTH INDIAN DAL Serves 4-6

## Ingredients

1½ cups orange lentils*          ¼ teaspoon garam masala*

1 teaspoon salt                  1 teaspoon toasted cumin seeds*

1 teaspoon turmeric*             2 tablespoons olive oil

1 teaspoon coriander powder*     1 medium onion, diced

1 teaspoon curry powder*         ½ cup fresh cilantro leaves

½ teaspoon chili powder*         ½ lemon

## Directions

1. Rinse the lentils until water runs clear. Place in a large pot and cover with two inches of water. Bring to a boil and add the salt and turmeric.

2. Reduce heat to medium-low and allow to simmer for 25-30 minutes. Meanwhile add the coriander, curry, chili, garam masala, toasted cumin seeds, and 1 tablespoon of olive oil to a pan and roast over medium-low heat for 2 minutes or until fragrant. Reserve spice mixture in a separate bowl.

3. In the same pan used for roasting the spices, add the diced onion and remaining tablespoon of oil. Cook onions until soft, about 10 minutes, then add the spice mixture to the onions and cook another minute. Add the onions and spice mixture to the lentils and let the flavors meld together for another 15 minutes.

4. Serve warm. Garnish with fresh cilantro leaves and a squeeze of fresh lemon juice.

## ROTI

## Ingredients

1 cup wheat flour          1 cup warm water

½ teaspoon salt            1 teaspoon butter or olive oil

## Directions

1. In a medium-size mixing bowl, combine flour and salt. Then slowly add the water in ¼-cup intervals, making a soft dough. If dough seems too wet, add a bit more flour to firm up.

2. Knead the dough a few times.

3. Separate the dough into 8 equal-size balls; each ball should be about 2 inches in diameter. You may want to add a small amount of oil to your hands so the dough won't stick.

4. On a floured surface, roll out the dough balls into 5-inch circles; add flour to the rolling pin as needed.

5. Heat a nonstick or cast-iron skillet for a few minutes over medium-high heat. When the pan is hot add the butter or oil. Ensure the butter or oil is evenly distributed; then put the first roti in the pan.

6. Cook on each side for about 2-3 minutes until the dough begins to brown and puff up. Set cooked roti on a plate and cover with paper towels to keep warm until it is time to serve.

Clockwise from top left: orderly Brazilian brigadeiros, waiting to be taken to a party; Fluff S'mores Brûlée, pre-folded Taza Chocolate Beignets; an Oreo cameo by Judith Klausner; Flufferettes at the What the Fluff? festival; Alberto Cabré, preparing Merengón de Fresa.

Olivia Peters

Dustin Kerstein

 COOKIE CAMEOS

 FLUFF S'MORES BRÛLÉE

 MERENGÓN DE FRESA

 TAZA CHOCOLATE BEIGNETS WITH COFFEE CRÈME ANGLAISE

 BRAZILIAN BRIGADEIRO

# COOKIE CAMEOS

## Local artist Judith Klausner finds her edible media at Union Square markets

Judith Klausner likes to play with her food. Yet the word "play" hardly conveys the curious and beautiful objets d'art she creates using edible media like Oreo cookies, Chex cereal and sliced bread. Judith is a 2011 Somerville Arts Council grant winner. Yet we are not the only ones who have noticed her talents. Her work has been exhibited at the Boston Museum of Fine Arts and the MIT Media Lab, and featured in the *Huffington Post, Harper's Magazine* and in blogs by *The Guardian* and *Bon Appetit*. Here, we present two of Klausner's pieces, both using sandwich cookies as a medium: one uses a classic Oreo cookie; the other uses a Crown cookie, a brand made in Korea and available at Reliable Market.

A cameo made with a Korean cookie found at Reliable Market.

Nibble: When did you start to use food as a medium for your art?

**Judith Klausner:** The original inspiration for the series came from looking at the "Kraft" brand name. I thought, "I wonder if I could make crafts with Kraft?" and it just kind of went from there. I've long explored unusual media, and I like to reinterpret the everyday. I'm interested in how the histories of both food and craft are bound up with gender—so combining these topics clicked for me.

Nibble: How does using food as a medium—specifically packaged food like Oreos and bread—lend meaning to your art?

**Judith:** My work is about choice. I consider myself a foodie; I love good, fresh food. I love to cook. But I also know that grabbing something pre-made gives me the time to do things like make art. I love old-fashioned clothes and Victorian furniture, but I also know that nostalgia can be dangerous. The key is to take the things we appreciate about the past and find ways to

A cameo made using an Oreo cookie.

integrate them into our contemporary way of life, while continuing to make strides towards equality.

Culturally, we have begun to rebel against ubiquitous mechanization, leading to resurgences in handcrafts and cooking. Within this atmosphere, the temptation to romanticize the past is strong. But this is a past where these handmade goods and from-scratch meals were the product of a society where women had no other options. The availability of packaged foods allows all of us the time to pursue careers, to develop new technologies, to create.

**Nibble: Your Oreo cameos are so delicate; how do you manage to carve them?**

**Judith:** I have always loved working on a small scale, and to be honest, Oreos are less delicate than insects! (I worked for a number of years with insects as a medium, and they are incredibly fragile.) As far as technique goes, I begin by garroting the top cookie off, using a piece of very thin wire. From there, I use toothpicks, a straight pin and a sculpture tool that is basically a small ball on a stick. I do the basic silhouette with the toothpicks, the finer detail with the pin, and then things like the area above the eye and next to the mouth with the sculpture tool. I use the heat from my finger to smooth—it comes in handy for this work that I have such small hands.

**Nibble: How did the Crown sandwich cookie from Korea work as a medium, compared to Oreo cookies?**

**Judith:** The creme in the Crown cookies was much harder to work with—it had a foamy texture that was difficult to shape and smooth. So, there aren't as many fine details on the Crown cameo. However, because the whole cookie was larger than an Oreo, it did give me room to include more large-scale details, like the necklace.

**Nibble: Did using a cookie that hails from Korea have any significance for you?**

**Judith:** It's interesting how small the differences are between these two products that come from opposite sides of the world. Ours has certainly become a global economy! Only a generation ago, it was incredibly difficult to find groceries from other countries. I feel lucky to have grown up at a time when I could experience foods from all over the world. I come from an eastern European family, but I was raised eating Indian pickles and Chinese sauces.

**Nibble: Has your recent cameo series increased or decreased your taste for Oreos?**

**Judith:** My tolerance for sugar has gone way down since I was a kid. I have to say, I haven't liked Oreos for many years—except in mint ice cream, where somehow they're still delicious! ●

# FLUFF S'MORES BRÛLÉE

**Two food historians offer a quick history of Fluff—inspiration for whipping up this flufferific brûlée!**

Fluff may be a twentieth-century invention, but its roots go back to the days of King Tut. Indeed, the marshmallow plant, *althaea officinalis*, was used 5,000 years ago by the Egyptians. A confection derived from the sap was used for medicinal purposes, and mixed with honey and nuts as a sweet. By the nineteenth century, the French sweetened the same substance by whipping it with sugar into a meringue and adding rose water. Later, the plant was discarded from the recipe. Today marshmallows are made with corn syrup, sugar, dried egg whites and vanilla.

In 1909, the *Ice Cream Trade Journal* advertised "Mallow Whipped Cream" as a "white superfine delicately flavored, scientifically made Marshmallow fondant; complying with the Pure Food Laws, and guaranteed to keep sweet and delicious under all conditions in all climates." This proto-Fluff was manufactured by the Mazetta Manufacturing Company in Chicago. But it was Somervillian Archibald Query who, in 1917, perfected his version, using a whipping method that made it especially "fluffy." Sold door-to-door by Query, his confection achieved early success, until thwarted by sugar rationing during World War I.

After the war, Query sold the recipe to two entrepreneurs, H. Allen Durkee and Fred L. Mower, who patented it. Inspired by their time in France during the war, the duo named the product Toot Sweet Marshmallow Fluff (an Americanized version of *tout de suite*, meaning "right now!"). Eventually, the moniker was shortened to Fluff. By the 1970s, the sticky stuff had become entirely Americanized. Smeared on bread with peanut butter, Fluff made its way into school cafeterias in the form of Fluffernutter sandwiches.

Since 2006, as part of the Somerville Arts Council's ArtsUnion Event Series, Union Square Main Streets has hosted the epically gooey What the Fluff? festival. In 2011, Jill Downer took home the festival's cooking contest grand prize—with good reason. Jill elevates the quotidian Fluff to a position of sophistication, reminding us of the French haute cuisine influence, while nodding to the Americana flavors of s'mores.

Recipe: **Jill Downer** | Text, Recipe Testing & Food Styling: **Beth Forrest and Deirdre Murphy** | Photography: **Olivia Peters** (unless otherwise noted)

# FLUFF S'MORES BRÛLÉE

Makes 8

## CRUST

### Ingredients:

2 cups graham cracker crumbs (about
   10 crackers)
½ cup butter, melted
3 tablespoons sugar
either: 8 teaspoons Nutella or a
Hershey's Bar (for traditionalists)

### Directions:

1. In a food processor, crumble
crackers if whole; then mix in melted
butter and sugar. Carefully press
mixture into bottom and up the sides of
8 6-inch ramekins.
2. Bake at 400°F for 10 minutes; cool.
3. Drop a teaspoon of Nutella or a
square of the Hershey's Bar into the
bottom of each ramekin.

Lynda and Jon Manganello drove down from New
Hampshire in full-on Fluff attire for Union Square's 2011
What the Fluff? festival.

Top: A crowd at the What the Fluff? fesival; below: a girl at the festival plays blindman's bluff, one of the many Fluff-themed games.

## BRÛLÉE

### Ingredients:
6 egg yolks
½ cup Marshmallow Fluff
1 quart heavy cream
1 teaspoon vanilla
sugar

### Directions:
1. Lower the oven to 325°F.
2. In a mixing bowl, combine the egg yolks with the Fluff and beat until smooth. Slowly incorporate the cream and vanilla into the egg mixture while whisking.
3. Pour into ramekins with the prepared crusts and place ramekins in a roasting pan.
4. Create a bain-marie, or water bath, by filling the roasting pan with hot water so that the level of water reaches at least halfway up the sides of the ramekins. Make sure that no water spills into the ramekins, or the custard will not set properly.
5. Bake for one hour or until the crème brûlées are set but still a bit wobbly in the middle.
6. Remove from bain-marie and refrigerate until cool (several hours or overnight).
7. To serve, sprinkle a thin layer of sugar over the top of the custards. Using a blowtorch or the broiler, caramelize the sugar (if you are using the broiler, be careful not to rewarm the custard; rechill if this becomes a problem).

# MERENGÓN DE FRESA

**From Casa B's fine wood-and-steel basement kitchen comes a delicious twist on a traditional Colombian dessert.**

Alberto Cabré of Casa B begins assembling a decidedly architectural merengón.

In many restaurants you often find a "dessert divide," resulting when chefs shy away from baking and focus on their entrées. Not so with Alberto Cabré, head chef and co-owner of Casa B in the heart of Union Square. "I love baking," he says. "It comes from my background in architecture. The careful measuring comes easily to me." In fact, the owners of Casa B—Alberto and his wife, Angelina Jockovich—are both trained architects.

This design background proved invaluable in opening their restaurant, which serves up creative Spanish and Caribbean food. Upstairs, the feel is airy and elegant yet homey. But the real transformation is downstairs, which features a "living wall"—a vertical garden packed with leafy green plants. In the stylish downstairs kitchen, Alberto continues comparing cuisine and architecture. "They both have process and method," he says. "With architecture you have walls and beams to create space. With cooking you have your ingredients, the fruits and vegetables, to create structure on the plate."

Alberto grew up cooking with his maternal grandfather, Ernesto Bobonis, who was a restaurant owner in San Juan, Puerto Rico. In fact, the "B" in "Casa B" signifies Bobonis. Yet when Alberto borrows his grandfather's recipes, he makes them his own, always adding a clever twist. He does this, in fact, with every dish he creates—whatever its origins. Take, for example, his Merengón de Fresa. Alberto bases this dessert on merengóns he sampled in Barranquilla, Colombia, Angelina's hometown. The difference between the classic dessert and Alberto's version is in the details: Alberto carefully marinates his fruit, and the plating is, not surprisingly, architectural.

Recipe: **Alberto Cabré** | Text: **Raleigh Strott** | Recipe Testing: **Bess Paupeck, Rachel Strutt** | Photography: Rachel Blumenthal

# MERENGÓN DE FRESA   Serves 4-6

## MERINGUE

### Ingredients
4 egg whites
1 cup white sugar
1 teaspoon vanilla (to taste)

### Directions
1. In a large bowl, whip egg whites until soft. Gradually add sugar, then vanilla. Continue to whip until mixture creates peaks when withdrawing the whisk or mixer.
2. Preheat oven to 225 degrees.
3. Prepare a baking tray: take a sheet of parchment paper, and trace 12 circles 3 to 4 inches in diameter on the back of the sheet in ballpoint pen. Place this paper ink side down on a baking sheet.
4. Put meringue in a piping bag (or light plastic bag; tie off the open end once full and clip one corner). Carefully pipe meringue to fill each circle on the parchment paper. You may need to flatten mixture with a spatula.
5. Bake meringue for 1 hour on middle shelf, do not brown.
6. Once baked, the meringue should have a thin crust and satiny shine. Cool and put in an airtight container.

*Shopping tip: Capone Foods has a great selection of balsamic vinegars; muscatel is available at Jerry's Liquors; and you can special-order crème fraîche at Sherman Market.
Recipe tip 1: You can skip the chocolate sauce and marinated bananas and your merengón will still dazzle.
Recipe tip 2: If you don't like desserts too sweet, add a little less sugar to the bananas and strawberries.

## MARINATED BANANAS

### Ingredients
1 large ripe banana, sliced in wheels about ¼ inch thick

2 tablespoons white sugar
2 tablespoons muscatel wine*

### Directions
1. Combine sliced bananas, sugar and muscatel in a bowl.
2. Mix ingredients thoroughly without mashing bananas.
3. Let the bananas sit for 2-3 hours in the refrigerator.

# MARINATED STRAWBERRIES

## Ingredients

10 strawberries, sliced thinly (¼ inch or less)
2 tablespoons white sugar
2 tablespoons high-quality balsamic vinegar*

## Directions

1. Combine sliced strawberries, sugar and balsamic vinegar in a bowl.
2. Mix ingredients thoroughly.
3. Let mixture sit for 2-3 hours (no longer) in the refrigerator.

# CHOCOLATE SAUCE

## Ingredients

1½ cups heavy cream
8 ounces of your favorite dark chocolate

## Directions

1. In a medium-sized, heavy-bottomed saucepan, heat cream over medium heat until bubbles gather at the edges of the pan.
2. Gradually add chocolate, stirring constantly.
3. Once mixture is blended, remove from heat.
4. Allow to cool and transfer to a squeeze bottle.

# WHIPPED CREAM

## Ingredients

1 cup heavy cream
3 tablespoons white sugar

½ teaspoon vanilla
1 cup crème fraîche*

## Directions

1. In a mixing bowl, whip cream and sugar together until stiff.
2. Add vanilla; then fold in crème fraîche.
3. Refrigerate until ready to serve.

## STRAWBERRY SAUCE

### Ingredients

6-8 strawberries, sliced
¼ cup white sugar
1 teaspoon cornstarch

½ cup white wine (chardonnay, sauvignon blanc, or your favorite)

### Directions

1. Combine all ingredients in a saucepan over low heat.
2. Cook until mixture is reduced by half, or 10-15 minutes.
3. Take care and stir frequently to avoid browning mixture.
4. Allow mixture to cool; move to a blender and purée.
5. Strain (optional) and refrigerate until ready to serve.

> **Recipe tip**: The strawberry sauce, chocolate sauce and meringue can be prepared in advance. Once you are comfortable with the recipe, experiment! Substitute different fruits or liqueurs, make meringue in different shapes; infuse your whipped cream with flavors. The possibilities are endless!

## MERENGÓN ASSEMBLY

*Note: If you want smaller portions, you can create 6 shorter merengóns, using only two meringues per plate.*

1. Spoon a tablespoon of strawberry reduction sauce onto a medium-sized round plate. Spread evenly with the back of the spoon until circle is about 5 or 6 inches in diameter.
2. Using squeeze bottle, draw a lattice of chocolate sauce across the strawberry sauce.
3. Place one piece of meringue on the plate.
4. Add one dollop of whipped cream (about 2 tablespoons); top with four slices of strawberries.
5. Add a second dollop of whipped cream and place another piece of meringue on top.
6. Place another dollop of cream, then 5 banana wheels.
7. Add another dollop of whipped cream, followed by a final piece of meringue.
8. Place a final dollop of whipped cream on top, then 4 slices of strawberries and one banana wheel. If you like, garnish with a sprig of mint.
9. Serve immediately.

Wooden spoons from Colombia adorn a wall downstairs at Casa B.

# TAZA CHOCOLATE BEIGNETS WITH COFFEE CRÈME ANGLAISE

**Before getting out your mixing bowl, here's a quick back story to Taza Chocolate, which gives these upscale confections their rustic flavor.**

Lucia Austria, who works in the Taza factory, presents a plate of beignets.

Alex Whitmore, co-founder of Taza Chocolate, discovered the pre-Columbian rituals related to *xocolatl* (drinking chocolate) while steeping himself in the culture of Oaxaca, Mexico. Enchanted with chocolate and its history, Alex decided to bring Mesoamerican-style chocolate to his hometown: Somerville. He studied under a *molinero*, a stone miller, and brought back *molinos* to replicate the granular texture found in Oaxacan chocolate.

Back home, he teamed up with Larry Slotnick, also a Taza co-founder. Together they developed a chocolate-making method that Taza still uses today. First, the raw cacao beans are roasted, then winnowed and ground; finally, the chocolate is molded into bars.

Although their chocolate is brown, this company sure is green. Taza's Direct Trade Certified cacao comes from small cooperatives in the Dominican Republic and Bolivia; their sugar is sourced from an innovative company in Brazil called the Green Cane Project; and they use true cinnamon (not the more common cascia) and whole vanilla pods, both organically grown, from a small plantation in Costa Rica. Most orders in the Metro Boston area are delivered via cargo trike by Somerville's own Metro Pedal Power.

Production Assistant Lucia Austria can't help but be inspired by the delicious offerings of the factory. An inventive baker, Lucia developed this recipe for chocolate-filled beignets in the "Taza Test Kitchen" and shared them with the staff. "They were a hit," says Lucia, who now makes them regularly. "I enjoy working with the yeast dough, kneading it out and watching it rise; it's almost magical." She pauses, then adds, "The wide-eyed look of astonishment and delight on your friends' faces when you bring out a heaping pile of hot beignets is reason enough to make them all the time!"

Recipe: Lucia Austria | Text: Elysian McNiff | Photography: Dustin Kerstein | Recipe Testing and Food Styling: Valeria Amato

# TAZA CHOCOLATE BEIGNETS WITH COFFEE CRÈME ANGLAISE

Makes about 3 dozen beignets

## GANACHE

### Ingredients

4 ounces Taza 70% baking squares*
½ cup heavy cream
2 tablespoons butter

*Shopping Tip**: Find Taza products at their factory store or at www.tazachocolate.com.

### Directions

Prepare the ganache first:

1. Heat the cream and butter in a small saucepan.
2. When it comes to a simmer, remove from the heat.
3. Gradually whisk in Taza squares until the mixture becomes thick and smooth.
4. Pour into a heatproof container and put in the refrigerator, uncovered, to solidify until ready for use.

# BEIGNETS
## (ADAPTED FROM PAULA DEEN)

## Ingredients

¾ cup lukewarm water
¼ cup granulated sugar
½ tablespoon (about ½ envelope) active dry yeast
1 egg
½ teaspoon salt
½ cup evaporated milk
3½ cups bread flour
2 tablespoons butter, softened
nonstick spray or vegetable oil
oil, for deep-frying (amount depends on size of your pan;
    you'll need at least 2-3 inches of oil)
1½ cups confectioners' sugar

## Directions

1. Mix water, sugar and yeast in a large bowl and let sit for 10 minutes.

2. In a bowl, beat the egg, salt and evaporated milk together.

3. Add egg mixture to the yeast mixture.

4. Add half the flour (about 1¾ cups) to the yeast mixture and stir to combine.

5. Add the butter and continue to stir while adding the remaining flour. Be sure to incorporate the butter throughout the mixture, breaking it up with your fingers as needed. (Depending on your brand of bread flour and the humidity of the room, your dough may require a little more or less than 3½ cups. The dough should be a bit sticky, but not wet.)

6. Remove dough from the bowl, place on a lightly floured surface and knead until smooth.

7. Spray a large bowl with nonstick spray or coat with a little vegetable oil.

8. Put dough in the bowl and cover with plastic wrap or a towel. Let rise in a warm place for at least 2 hours. (While the dough rests, you can make the crème anglaise.)

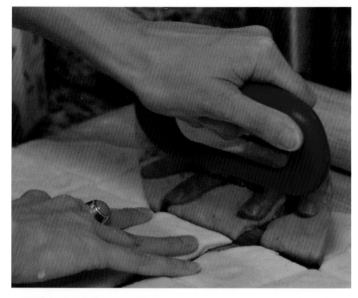

# COFFEE CRÈME ANGLAISE
## (ADAPTED FROM EMERIL LAGASSE)

## Ingredients
1½ cups brewed high quality coffee*, boiled down
and reduced to approximately ⅓ cup
¾ cup heavy cream
¾ cup whole milk
⅓ cup granulated sugar
3 egg yolks
1 teaspoon Taza Mexicano extract*

## Directions
1. Heat the cream and milk in a 2-quart saucepan over medium heat.
2. Meanwhile, in a medium-sized mixing bowl, combine the sugar and the egg yolks and beat until well blended and pale yellow in color.
3. Once the cream and milk come to a simmer, remove from the heat and slowly pour about ½ cup of the cream and milk mixture over the eggs; whisk to blend.
4. Return the saucepan to the stove, and add the egg-cream mixture.
5. Stir the mixture with a wooden spoon, making sure to reach the corners of the pan.
6. Continue to stir until the anglaise begins to thicken and coats the back of the spoon, about 5 minutes.
7. Once thickened, remove from the heat and strain into a clean bowl using a fine mesh sieve.
8. Add the Taza Mexicano extract and the reduced coffee to the anglaise and stir to combine.

**Recipe Tip**: Lucia likes Counter Culture coffee, which is flavored with chicory.

## BEIGNET ASSEMBLY
1. Preheat oil in a heavy-bottom pan or deep fryer to 350°F. If you're frying in a pan, you'll need at least 2-3 inches of oil.
2. Line a large plate or baking dish with paper towels
3. Take the cooled ganache out of the refrigerator. It should be solid, yet still soft.
4. On a lightly floured surface, roll the dough out to about ⅛-inch thickness and cut into 3-inch squares.
5. Place a little less than a teaspoon of ganache on one half of each square, leaving a little bit of space at the edge.
6. Fold the other half of the square over the ganache, making sure to pinch the sides tightly to prevent the chocolate from seeping out during frying.
7. Working in batches, fry the beignets, flipping constantly, until they become a golden color. Don't crowd the pan or fryer with too many beignets, otherwise the oil temperature will get too low and the beignets will be greasy.
8. After beignets are fried, drain them for a minute or two on paper towels, and dust them generously with sifted confectioners' sugar. Serve with a side of the crème anglaise for dipping.

# BRAZILIAN BRIGADEIRO

**Elizabete Delfino shares her recipe for these addictive chocolate treats.**

Elizabete Delfino, flanked by Kathleen Hennessey (left) and Rachel Strutt.

Elizabete Delfino's house feels cozy as the smell of pão de queijo (Brazilian cheese popovers) emanates from the oven. Pão de queijo is a specialty of Minas Gerais—the Brazilian state where Elizabete and roughly 75 percent of Brazilians living in Somerville come from. So Elizabete knows this recipe well. In fact, she could whip up a batch in her sleep, along with other classic Brazilian dishes she cooks for her family, like feijão e arroz (rice and beans), salpicão (chicken salad) and pastel de camarão (shrimp-filled pastry).

Food brings people together, which is what she loves. "Back in Brazil, there were many days when my mother, aunts, cousins and I would get together to clean and cook for the main meal at noon," Elizabete recalls. "Sometimes we would have barbecues that lasted all day long! Other days, we spent the afternoons talking to neighbors on the stairs, keeping an eye on the kids, drinking coffee and telling stories."

Elizabete misses the happy and laid-back lifestyle of Brazil, but says that things are easier here—especially when it comes to cooking. In this country, ingredients like shredded coconut are cheap and readily available at local stores like Pão de Açúcar and Market Basket. Whereas back in Brazil, Elizabete would buy a whole coconut, break it, and grate the meat because the prepared version was too expensive.

As Elizabete pulls out a tattered and beloved 23-year-old recipe book to show us the brigadeiro recipe, she explains that the key to success with these sweet treats is taking your time. If you stir constantly and wait until the mixture is the ideal temperature before forming the balls, your patience will yield success. Shredded coconut is just one of the toppings you can use for brigadeiros. Also consider crushed pretzels or toffee bars—or add cinnamon or a dash of Bailey's to the mix. These chocolate balls make great presents and are perfect for parties. In fact, Elizabete tells us that in Brazil, "a party isn't a party without brigadeiros!"

Recipe and Food Styling: **Elizabete Delfino** | Text: **Kathleen Hennessey** | Photography: **Dustin Kerstein** | Recipe Testing: Lisa Young

**Recipe tip**: Try not to eat them the same day! Brigadeiros are best once they are slightly hardened—around two days standing—and stay fresh for a week or more.
**Shopping tip**: The wrappers we used here are available at Kerr Party Decoration, 361 Somerville Avenue, in Union Square.

# BRIGADEIRO   Makes 40

## Ingredients

1 can of condensed milk (Moca or Itampe brand; Elizabete prefers Moca)
2 teaspoons butter
4 tablespoons Nesquik or other cocoa powder
¼ cup regular milk
chocolate sprinkles or toppings of your choice, like crushed pretzels

## Directions

1. Mix condensed milk, 1 teaspoon butter and cocoa powder together gradually in a thick pan. Once mixed, stir in regular milk.
2. Beginning on high heat, bring the mixture to a boil, stirring constantly.
3. Once boiling, reduce heat to medium and continue stirring; simmer for 5 minutes, or until batter is thick enough to hold a line drawn by a wooden spoon.
4. Remove from heat; stir in 1 teaspoon butter and allow mixture to cool completely in a greased bowl.
5. Once batter has cooled completely and before it starts to soften too much (may take an hour or so), grease your hands and roll batter into balls roughly one inch in diameter.
6. Roll balls in chocolate sprinkles or toppings of your choice.

This page, clockwise from left: sesame-encrusted tofu triangles and pork meatballs; a raucous scene at 2011's Hungry Tiger Street Food Festival; Bartender Thea Engst presents "The Union" at the Independent; ceviche with ají amarillo; Somerville Arts Council Director Gregory Jenkins underneath a local grape arbor. Facing page: Roberto Rendón, inventor of exotic margaritas—fig flavor, jalapeño, cactus, the list goes on!

Dustin Kerstein

Rachel Strutt

# Wine, Cocktails & Nibbles

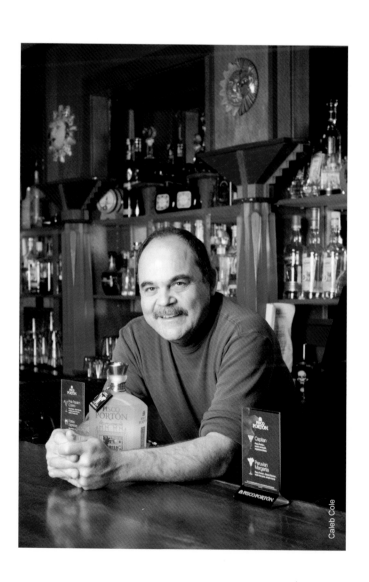

Caleb Cole

 URBAN VINEYARDS

 WORLD PARTY

 THE UNION & POLENTA ROUNDS WITH ROASTED TOMATO JAM AND CHORIZO

 CURRIED SCALLOP CAKES WITH CILANTRO PESTO & THE MAHARAJA'S REVENGE

 PERÚ NEGRO & CEVICHE WITH AJÍ AMARILLO

 PORK MEATBALLS WITH A SOY- WASABI SAUCE & SEOUL KISS

# URBAN VINEYARDS

**Two local grape growers—one from the Azores, the other from Portugal—harvest their vines each fall to make gallons and gallons of wine.**

By Gregory Jenkins | Photography by Rachel Strutt

Manuel Borges (right) poses with his daughter Sheila and grandson Bobby for a family portrait at the Neighborhood.

The current enthusiasm for gardening, local food and community-supported agriculture reminds me of growing up in rural North Carolina during the '70s, when gardening, hunting and fishing were part of everyday life. Nearly every neighbor had a garden. I remember one friend had old apple trees. When they occasionally bore fruit, we'd pick, peel, and core them to make pies. They tasted pretty good, and it didn't make sense to let anything go to waste.

Thirty years later, I'm living in Somerville, one of the most densely populated cities in the country. Over the years, I've been impressed by the small gardens with oversized ambition. You see modest plots bursting with tomatoes, herbs and flowers. And you see a surprising number of grape arbors, often tucked away in backyards or perched above driveways.

An especially spectacular local arbor is found in Union Square at the Neighborhood Restaurant, owned by the Borges family, who live in a few apartments upstairs from their eatery. Its 1,600 square feet form a verdant roof for outdoor diners in summer months. The arbor comprises four vines—two are Concord grapes, the other two are white grapes. When Manuel Borges bought the property in 1980, a few vines were already growing; he has replaced some over the years, but at least one of the vines is over 30 years old.

Manuel Borges, or Manny as he's known, is a nonagenarian who still works daily at the family restaurant, which serves Portuguese fare like bacalhau assado (broiled cod) and hearty breakfasts that include herb-tinged sausages and a delicious cream of wheat. Borges, who speaks only a little English, hails from the Azores, a volcanic archipelago 1,000 miles off the coast of Portugal. He was born on the island of São Miguel, known as the "green island" because of its fertile soils. As an adult, he and his wife moved to the States, first to Newark, New Jersey, and then, in 1980, to Somerville.

Each fall, Borges makes wine from his grapes. "These grapes aren't the best for wine," he explains. "They're not like California grapes, but only Concord grapes survive here." Each season he makes between 30 to 50 quarts of both red and white wine. Both varieties are light and sweet and don't keep long. Manny, who learned how to make wine from an Italian friend named Cosmos, likes to share his wine with family and friends.

Like many other local winemakers, Borges buys some California Burgundy grapes to mix with his Concord grapes when making red wine. The winemaking is straightforward: the grapes are crushed in large blue containers, then covered and left for three days. Then Borges stirs them again and lets them sit another three to four weeks. In addition to wine, Borges makes four to five gallons of grape jelly each fall. "If we don't use all the grapes, they would all go to waste," he says. "And I don't want to waste anything."

Manuel Borges takes a break underneath the grape arbor at his family's restaurant, the Neighborhood. At his side is one of the many jugs of wine he makes each fall.

Similar to many Somerville gardens, every square foot of the Borges' plot is used for growing produce. Along the perimeter of the arbor are gardens brimming with basil, rosemary, parcel (leaf celery) and, occasionally, tomatoes. Borges' grandson Mario, who is always translating and augmenting his grandfather's responses, chimes in, "He likes to plant things; he likes herbs, he enjoys himself out here. Plus, he says he wants to leave it for us."

On an early spring day each year, another Manny appears underneath the Neighborhood's grape arbor: Manuel DaSilva, a viticulture expert who hails from Britelo, Portugal. He shows up with pruning shears, string, and little more, and within minutes is clipping vines, tying back last year's shoots to the new year's branches, then cutting off the "third" year branches. "You've got to prune them before they start to bud," says DaSilva, who gives his age as near 60.

When DaSilva was 16, he got a job building trellises at a rural Portuguese vineyard and soon learned how to prune. Although he only had this job for two years, he never forgot these skills or his love of physical outdoor work. These days, at his Medford house, a stone's throw from Somerville, DaSilva keeps his own arbor in impeccable shape. As he climbs a ladder to pull off leaves, he says that there is little work after the initial spring pruning—just thinning leaves. This allows more sunlight in, which increases the grapes' sugar content.

When the vines don't need attention, DaSilva finds countless other ways to keep busy. In addition to his arbor—comprising three Concord vines and one white grape vine that emerge from small holes in the paved driveway—the property is packed to the gills with mint, basil, tomatoes and flowers. There is no room for grass, only garden, and seemingly every inch is utilized and lovingly tended. When DaSilva runs out of gardening chores at home, he often migrates into neighbors' gardens to work on various projects. "I love being outside and I like helping my friends," he says matter-of-factly. "He keeps himself busy!" his daughter Theresa chimes in.

Both the Somerville and Medford Mannys not only embrace hard work, they enjoy squeezing abundant produce from their urban plots. This common-sense mentality reminds me of those hardscrabble apples in North Carolina. It's not about making award-winning pies or wines, it's about that rural ethos of using the land, however big or small the plot, and putting its bounty to good use.

—*Gregory Jenkins is the executive director at the Somerville Arts Council.* ●

Left: Manuel DaSilva, with his daughter, Theresa; right: Manuel picks leaves to allow more light to reach the grapes, which raises their sugar level.

# WORLD PARTY

**Two globetrotters—a cocktail wizard and the best cook we know—have concocted cocktails and accompanying nibbles to represent the global flavor of Union Square.**

Brother Cleve and Julie Betters

Yes, indeed, mixologist Brother Cleve—who is also a musician, DJ, the list goes on—has concocted four cocktails especially for our beloved square. To sample one such drink, stroll into the Independent and ask for the "Union." Or, try stirring things up at home and make it a party! Because any worthy cocktail soirée requires fun finger food, we asked Julie Betters—who has worked as a personal chef and taken cooking classes in Thailand, Bali, Laos, and Mexico—to create a complementary nibble for each libation. Okay, buckle up: over to Cleve and Julie.

**Cleve:** This quartet of original cocktails represents the past, present and future of Union Square—and all of Somerville. In the past several decades, new immigrants have entered the city: Brazilians, Haitians, Koreans, Pakistanis, Nepalis, Peruvians, Guatemalans—importing with them the flavors of their homelands. They have joined the earlier waves of Irish, Italians and Portuguese who built Somerville in the 19th and 20th centuries. Together, these immigrants have made Somerville the city that it is today. *Spirit*-tually speaking, immigrants have brought whiskey, wine, Port, Madeira, cachaça, rum, aguardiente, pisco, amaro, beer, sake and soju to the Somerville table.

In the past 25 years, we've witnessed change in the 'ville's drinking landscape. It was once a city filled with divey "old man" bars. Today, family-run ethnic eateries with liquor licenses share the scene with cool contemporary cocktail lounges—like Union Square's new backbar, for example—and, thankfully, some of those great old dive bars remain. I wish we had room here to indulge in more spirited beverages influenced by our neighbors from Brazil, Haiti, Guatemala, Colombia and Thailand. But for now, experience all that our city has to offer, and never be afraid to sample a beverage, intoxicating or not. It could become your new favorite libation!

**Julie:** The perfect steak with a glass of merlot. Fish tacos and an icy Pacifico. Champagne and caviar—the pairing of food and drink is important business. When I was asked to take four unique cocktails and match them with four original nibbles, I was excited to put my many years of eating, drinking and globetrekking to the test.

As it turns out, producing the perfect union takes some work. There were several tastings, revisions, and final decisions to be made before the sip of a cocktail and a bite of a little yum were in harmony. Each one of these pairings is designed to take you on a mini journey; rest assured that we've done our part to make sure it's a good trip.

Recipes: Brother Cleve (cocktails) and Julie Betters (nibbles) | Photography: Dustin Kerstein (unless otherwise noted) Recipe Testing: Ellen Kramer, Rachel Strutt, Flinn Metternick, Alex Buchanan, Katherine Perry | Glassware: Boston Shaker, 69 Holland Street, Davis Square

Rachel Strutt

## THE UNION

**Cleve:** This drink, which includes Irish whiskey, Portuguese Madeira and Italian amaro (an herbal digestivo), is a tribute to Somerville's initial immigrants. I call it the Union for a number of reasons. First up, it's a variation of the Manhattan, a cocktail that dates back to 1873. In recent years, this classic has been modified and renamed throughout New York City and Brooklyn: there's a "Red Hook," a "Carroll Gardens," a "Brooklyn Heights"—and many more. Continuing in this tradition, now there's a neighborhood drink for Union Square. The cocktail is a "new school" remix using classic "old school" Somerville spirits.

## Ingredients

2 ounces Irish whiskey
1 ounce medium dry Madeira wine
½ ounce Meletti Amaro
1 dash Angostura bitters
1 dash Angostura Orange bitters

## Directions

Combine all ingredients with ice in a mixing glass, and stir. Strain into a cocktail glass and garnish with a maraschino cherry.

*Shopping tip: All cocktail ingredients are available at Jerry's Liquors. The Union is now being served at the Independent.

# POLENTA ROUNDS WITH ROASTED TOMATO JAM AND CHORIZO  Makes 12

**Julie:** For the Union, I wanted to combine classic Mediterranean ingredients while maintaining distinct flavors. Polenta and tomatoes nod to Italy; chorizo nods to Portugal. Each bite and sip of this pairing will transform your kitchen into a cosy tapas bar.

## POLENTA ROUNDS

### Ingredients

1½ cups water
½ cup of chicken vegetable stock
1 cup polenta
¼ teaspoon white pepper
½ teapsoon salt
⅓ cup Parmesan cheese
½ cup chopped chorizo*

### Directions

1. Pour water and stock into a pot and bring to a boil. Add polenta, white pepper and salt and stir until it becomes thick, about 10 mintues. Just before you take it off the heat stir in the Parmesan.
2. Pour cooked polenta into an 8-by-8-inch baking dish and chill in the refrigerator for at least 1 hour.
3. When polenta is set, take a 2-inch round cookie cutter and cut out rounds of polenta and place on a cookie sheet. Press scraps together to form another sheet and cut out additional rounds.
4. Put the oven on broil. Place cookie sheet on top oven rack, in the highest position, and broil polenta until the tops brown.
5. Cut one slice of chorizo for each polenta round.
6. Heat a frying pan and cook chorizo slices for 1-2 minutes; set on a paper towel. Dice each slice of chorizo.
7. Top each round of polenta with tomato jam (at room temperature) and chorizo.

## TOMATO JAM

### Ingredients

10 medium tomatoes
2 tablespoons olive oil
salt and pepper

### Directions

1. Bring a large pot of water to a boil.
2. Put a cross hatch on the top of each tomato and drop in boiling water for 30-40 seconds. Remove and peel each tomato.
3. Slice tomatoes into ¼-inch-thick slices and layer the bottom of a 9-by12-inch baking dish; drizzle with olive oil and sprinkle liberally with salt and pepper
4. Bake at 375º for 40 minutes or until edges start to caramelize.
5. Use a spatula to remove the roasted tomatoes and put into a bowl; stir and drizzle with a little olive oil.

# CURRIED SCALLOP CAKE WITH CILANTRO PESTO

## SCALLOP CAKE  Serves 4-6, depending on size

### Ingredients

1 dozen sea scallops
1 teaspoon mayonnaise
½ teaspoon mustard powder
1 egg
1½ teaspoons curry powder*

1 tablespoon chopped cilantro
½ cup panko, and a little more
   for coating the cakes*
salt and pepper to taste

### Directions

1. Chop the scallops finely, put in a bowl and add the mayonnaise, mustard, egg, curry powder, panko, cilantro, salt and pepper.
2. Mix well and form 4 or 6 cakes. Put cakes in refrigerator for 1 hour.
3. Pour panko onto a plate and coat each side of cakes with panko.
4. In a frying pan, add enough canola oil to cover the bottom. When oil is hot, add the scallop cakes and fry until each side is browned, about 5 minutes per side. Try not to turn over more than once.

**Julie:** Rum always has been one of my favorite spirits. Its spicy sweetness provides a wonderful jumping off point for something warm and aromatic—curry.
Mix with the plump, delicately-flavored scallops, a spoonful of an unexpected pesto, and you have the perfect global comfort food.

**Recipe tip**: If you have time, make your own curry powder! See recipe on page 68.
*****Shopping tip**: Find panko at Reliable Market and other Asian markets.

## CILANTRO PESTO

### Ingredients

1 cup cilantro
½ cup unsweetened
   coconut flakes, toasted
½ cup almonds, toasted
½ cup olive oil
½ cup canola oil

1 tablespoon lemon juice
1 garlic clove
1 inch of a serrano pepper
¼ teaspoon salt
¼ teaspoon pepper

### Directions

1. Toast almonds and coconut in a toaster oven or broiler (toast them separately and be careful not to burn).
2. Place almonds, garlic and serrano pepper in a food processor; blend.
3. Add cilantro, blend; add coconut, blend; add lemon juice, blend.
4. Slowly pour olive oil slowly into food processor; blend until you have a paste.
5. Do the same with the canola oil (add a bit more than ½ cup if you like).
6. Add salt and pepper and blend.

# THE MAHARAJA'S REVENGE

**Cleve:** A few years ago my band had a record deal in my favorite country in the world: India! While touring there, I learned of the joys of Old Monk Indian rum. People may associate rum with the Caribbean, yet sugarcane is actually indigenous to southern Asia. In the sixteenth century, the British, who controlled India at the time, brought sugar to the Caribbean; this is where rum was first distilled. It was in 1855 that the first batch of Old Monk rum was produced in India. But I digress! Once I returned from India, I convinced the folks at Jerry's Liquors in Union Square to order Old Monk; now they carry it regularly. I base this cocktail on a pre-Prohibition libation known as the Millionaire #3. After a few you'll feel like a princely maharaja! Although the next morning, you may feel like a lowly *kisaan* (that's Hindi for "peasant"). That's the revenge.

## Ingredients
1½ ounces Old Monk rum
¾ ounce apricot liqueur
½ ounce fresh-squeezed lime juice

## Directions
Combine all ingredients with ice in a Boston shaker. Shake and strain into a cocktail glass. Garnish with a lime wheel.

# PERÚ NÉGRO

**Cleve:** The Peruvians make a spectacular brandy called pisco (the Chileans also make it, but quite differently). It's best known for the Pisco sour or pisco punch, though I've found pisco to be an incredibly versatile spirit. This is my Peruvian take on a Negroni cocktail. Perú Négro refers to a style of black Peruvian music enjoyed by descendants of African slaves—many of whom picked grapes to make pisco. It's a cyclical world, don't you know. Today, Perú Négro is the name of a contemporary Peruvian band reviving this music. And now it's also the name of this drink.

## Ingredients
1 ounce Macchu Pisco
1 ounce Campari
1 ounce Punt e Mes Italian vermouth
½ ounce Amaro Nonino
2 dashes Bittermens Xocalatl Molé bitters

## Directions
Combine all ingredients with ice in a mixing glass, and stir. Strain into an old-fashioned rocks glass. Garnish with a fat orange peel.

# "CEVICHE" WITH AJÍ AMARILLO  Serves 4

**Julie:** Native to Peru, ceviche holds exotic allure—and its bold citrus tang, chili heat and fresh seafood flavors represent summer. Of course ceviche is traditionally "cooked" using citrus juice. My version, however, uses grilled shrimp, which creates a firmer texture and a more developed flavor. The ají amarillo pepper is a key ingredient of Peruvian cuisine and adds a dash of color. One bite and Lima doesn't feel all that far away.

## Ingredients
½ cup ají amarillo pepper paste*
1 teaspoon sugar
3 tablespoons olive oil
juice of 2 limes
1 dozen medium shrimp, peeled and deveined
¼ red bell pepper, diced
slivered red onion to taste
1 ripe avocado, diced
⅓ cup cooked corn, cooled
about 2 tablespoons fresh cilantro
½-inch piece of a serrano pepper, chopped finely
kosher salt
1 bag plantain strips*

## Directions
1. Combine the ají amarillo in a food processor with the sugar, olive oil and juice of ½ lime to make a paste.
2. Marinate the shrimp in the paste; refrigerate for 1 hour.
3. Remove shrimp from marinade and grill—on the barbecue or using a grill pan—about 2 minutes each side. Chop into large pieces. Discard marinade.
4. With the exception of plantain strips, add all the remaining ingredients, including juice of 1½ limes, in a bowl; mix well.
5. Spoon into a martini glass or other small bowl and garnish with a plantain chip.

**\*Shopping tip**: These ingredients are found at La Internacional and other Latino markets.

# PORK MEATBALLS WITH SOY-WASABI SAUCE

Makes about 15 small meatballs

**Julie**: The key to working with gin's flavor profile—with its strong juniper notes—is taking it head on. After a few experiments, I found that this dish, with its wasabi dipping sauce, is a worthy opponent to gin's juniper. This cocktail-nibble pairing will make your mouth come alive with flavor.

## PORK MEATBALLS

### Ingredients

⅓ cup finely chopped shiitake mushrooms*
⅓ cup finely chopped red onion
½ pound ground pork
2 tablespoons soy sauce
1 teaspoon sesame oil
6-8 fresh finely chopped spinach leaves
1 teaspoon grated fresh ginger
salt and pepper
3 teaspoons canola oil

### Directions

1. Sauté the mushrooms and onion in 1 teaspoon canola oil until the onion is translucent, about 5 minutes; let cool.
2. In a large mixing bowl, add the pork, soy sauce, sesame oil, spinach, ginger, salt, pepper and cooled mushrooms and onion. Mix well and form into small meatballs.
3. In a large frying pan, over medium heat, pour enough canola oil—a few teaspoons—to cover the bottom. When the oil is hot, add the meatballs and brown.
4. Remove from the frying pan and place in an oven-safe baking dish. Bake at 350ºF for about 15-20 minutes.
5. Serve with the soy-wasabi dipping sauce.

**\*Shopping tip:** Find shiitake mushrooms at Sherman Market; find wasabi at Reliable Market and other Asian markets.

## SOY-WASABI DIPPING SAUCE

### Ingredients

⅓ cup soy sauce
1 full teaspoon prepared wasabi* (or more if you like it hot)

### Directions

Mix the 2 ingredients and serve alongside the meatballs.

## SEOUL KISS

**Cleve:** The Japanese and the Koreans both make a fermented rice beverage that is, technically, both a wine and a beer. Japan has its sake and Korea has soju, which is traditionally made with rice yet often includes other grains, including sweet potatoes, tapioca, and, sometimes, barley. This cocktail riffs on the classic martini, yet uses the sweeter Old Tom gin. This varietal was popular in the United States when the martini was first created in the 1880s; after an 80-year absence, it's available again! The secret ingredient here is the lesser-known blanc (or bianco) vermouth—a semisweet white vermouth with a flavor between the usual dry white and sweet red vermouths. 건 배, or rather, cheers!

## Ingredients
2 ounces Old Tom gin
¾ ounce Chum-Churum Soju
　(available at the Reliable Market)
½ ounce blanc or bianco style vermouth
2 dashes Fee Brothers Grapefruit
　bitters

## Directions
Combine all ingredients with ice in a mixing glass, and stir. Strain into a champagne coupe glass. Garnish with a melon ball.

**More at NIbble:** If you're looking for a great vegetarian nibble to accompany the Seoul Kiss, head to the recipe section at www.somervilleartscouncil.org/nibble and look for Sesame Encrusted Tofu Triangles with a Miso Glaze (below).

## Markets & Food Producers

### Capone Foods

14 Bow St. | 617.629.2296 | www.caponefoods.com
Hours: Mon-Fri, 8am-6pm; Sat, 10am-5pm; Sun, 12pm-5pm
Owners/from: Al Capone and Jennifer Hegarty, Argentina
Most customers hail from: Somervillians and restaurant buyers
What you'll find: Fresh pasta, homemade sauces, prepared meals, desserts, cheeses
Don't miss: Cooking classes (see their Web site for details)

In the back kitchen of Capone's, a machine dubbed "the Extruder" pumps out anywhere between 200–300 pounds of fresh pasta per day. Over 20 specialty pastas are available, including such enticing flavors as saffron, wild mushroom, squid ink and co-owner Jennifer Hegarty's favorite: rosemary and garlic. Pair any of these pastas with one of Capone's homemade sauces; ask for the pairing chart, which suggests delicious combos. Most of the recipes at Capone's were handed down from Al Capone's mother, Nina, or developed by Al himself. The store also stocks an impressive selection of olive oils and vinegars, as well as make-your-own cannoli kits—serve them at your next dinner party and pretend you made them from scratch.
—Sharon Wolfson & Rachel Strutt

### Casa de Carnes Solução

38 Bow St. | 617.625.1787
Hours: Mon-Thu, 8am-8pm; Fri-Sat, 8am-9pm; Sun, 8am-7pm
Owner/from: Edson Nascimento, Brazil
Most customers hail from: Brazil, Africa, Latin America and Somerville
What you'll find: Great cuts of meat and everything you need for a Brazilian BBQ, including top-quality sirloin, charcoal and seasoning
Don't miss: Chicken sausage

At this Brazilian-style butcher, you'll find not only meat, but also Brazilian staples and sweets, such as Garoto chocolates and a candy called Paçoquinha, made with peanuts. Casa de Carnes also sells juices and concentrates of superfruits açaí and acerola (also known as Barbados cherry, a tropical fruit native to the West Indies and northern South America). Edson is investing in a fruit concentrate, called polpa de pequi, made from pequi, a fruit native to the Brazilian Cerrado, a vast tropical savanna region in central Brazil. —Sharon Wolfson

From left to right: meat at Casa de Carnes; Heather Schmidt of Cuisine en Locale, located at Kitchen Inc.; EH Chocolatier bonbons.

## EH Chocolatier

561 Windsor St. B-206 | 617.284.6096 | www.ehchocolatier.com
Where to find it: Dave's Fresh Pasta, 81 Holland St., Somerville or order online
Owners/from: Elaine Hsieh (New York) and Catharine Sweeney (Wisconsin)
What you'll find: Artisan chocolates
Don't miss: Chocolate-making classes (see their Web site)

Many years ago Elaine Hsieh and Catharine Sweeney came together to create a wedding cake for a mutual friend. Baking together was a great experience, but at the time, they were immersed in other careers. But in 2011, the duo launched a chocolate company and started making confections full-time—handcrafted bonbons often tinged with spices and teas. These Somerville-based chocolatiers use top-notch ingredients for their artful chocolates, including Michel Cluizel and Valrhona chocolate from France, as well as Taza chocolate, the business conveniently located next door! You can purchase their products online (delivery or pick-up) or at the following stores: Formaggio Kitchen in Cambridge; South End Formaggio in Boston; City Feed and Supply in Jamaica Plain; Fastachi in Watertown; and Dave's Fresh Pasta in Somerville. —*Raleigh Strott*

## Fiore di Nonno

561 Windsor St. | www.fioredinonno.com
Where to find it: Sherman Market or Swirl and Slice (see page 121)
Owner/from: Lourdes Smith, Hoboken, New Jersey
What you'll find: Small-batch mozzarella made fresh daily, string cheese, stracciatella, burrata
Don't miss: Mascarpone Burrata, a combination of Italian mascarpone cheese and Greek yogurt wrapped in fresh mozzarella

As a child, owner Lourdes Smith adored her Italian grandfather's store, Fiore's of Hoboken. Inspired by memories of his fresh mozzarella, Smith tested batch after batch until she rediscovered the perfect recipe. Now a thriving business that supplies restaurants, retailers and farmers' markets throughout the Boston area, Fiore di Nonno not only produces superb mozzarella but also string cheese and rich, soft stracciatella, made with fresh cream and strings of mozzarella curds. Thanks to Smith's experiments with bold, sweet and savory flavoring, you'll find that Fiore di Nonno now makes burrata with mascarpone- and yogurt-based fillings such as Fig, Honey Lavender & Chili, and Za'atar, a Middle Eastern spice mixture. —*Sarah Champion*

## Kitchen Inc.

201 Somerville Ave. | 617.765.0433 | www.kitcheninc.com
Hours: By appointment
What it is: A culinary incubator housing several food businesses included Cuisine en Locale, Culinary Cruisers and the Bearded Pig Catering

The culinary incubator model is spreading across the country and Kitchen Inc. provides a local example. Many small food industry start-ups might not have the funds for a kitchen all to themselves, yet sharing a space for cooking and production resolves this issue. Kitchen Inc. is home to Michael Schmidt's Bearded Pig Catering, which cooks up classic Southern barbecue. Another resident business is Cuisine En Locale, a locavore catering outfit helmed by J. J. Gonson, which home-delivers meals (carnivore or vegetarian options) for an entire week for $125. Kitchen Inc. also includes Culinary Cruisers, a team revolutionizing the growing mobile food phenomena by delivering treats from kombucha to popsicles on bicycles! The space also offers kitchen time for occasional users and events. —*Raleigh Strott*

## La Internacional Foods

318 Somerville Avenue | 617.776.1880
Hours: Mon-Sat, 8am-9pm; Sun, 9am-7pm
Owners/from: Nora and Byron Cabrera, Guatemala
Most customers hail from: Haiti and Central and South America
What you'll find: Plantains, rice, spices, fish and produce from Costa Rica and Colombia
Don't miss: Assortment of dried chilies including pasilla, ancho and guajillo, djon djon mushrooms from Haiti

Customers come from as far away as Waltham, Mattapan and Malden for La Internacional's broad selection of Latin American and Haitian goods—and great prices. The store has so many Haitian customers that Byron has learned Haitian Kreyol just from talking with the clientele! Nora estimates that they sell a thousand 10-pound bags of rice each week. Check out the selection of spices, which includes numerous varieties of chili powder, including chile mulato and chile poblano. This is also the place to go for authentic tortillas, queso fresco and crema, as well as Salvadoran products like flor de izote and loroco. As for Haitian items, you'll find rare djon djon mushrooms, yams, yucca and drinks like cornmeal-based Akasan. —*Rachel Strutt*

## Little India

438 Somerville Ave. | 617.623.1786
Hours: Mon-Sat, 8am-9:30pm; Sun, 8am-8:30pm
Owners/from: Dipti and Umesh Mistri, Mumbai, India
Most customers hail from: Bangladesh, Pakistan and India, primarily the Punjab region
What you'll find: Spices, rice, fresh produce including bitter melon and daikon radishes
Don't miss: Ladu—round sweet balls made of wheat, lentils, ghee and sugar

Here you'll find a wide assortment of rice, including both white and brown basmati and the aromatic sona masuri variety. The Mistris also sell spices galore, including mustard seed, pomegranate powder, amchoor (green mango) powder and black and green cardamom. Ask Dipti Mistri about the medicinal value of spices and produce and she will offer you a wealth of information. For example, bitter melon is good for diabetes, and turmeric is excellent for colds and putting on cuts. Each October and November, Little India shoppers will also find sweet delicacies and decorations for Diwali, the Hindu New Year. The store also carries wine and beer, including many Indian brews. —Sharon Wolfson

## New Bombay Market

359 Somerville Ave. | 617.623.6614
Hours: Daily, 9am-10pm
Owner/from: Hari Prasad Lamichhane, Nepal
Most customers hail from: Nepal
What you'll find: Spices, lentils, dal, pickles
Don't miss: Sweet lapsi

Hailing from Katmandu, Nepal, Hari Prasad Lamichhane stocks his store with specialties of his homeland, including different forms of sweet lapsi, a dried fruit also known as hog plum that is used in achars (pickles) and sweet spicy candy. While you're there, take a whiff of the gorgeously fragrant spice timur, which looks like peppercorns and is used in achars (see recipe on page 58).The store also carries products like papadam, dal (udad, chana and moong varieties), gram flour (made from dal) and dried peas. The extensive spice collection includes star anise, amchoor powder and methi seed. Lamichhane explains that although over 80 percent of Nepal's population is engaged in agriculture, it is often much cheaper to import products from India, which, unlike Nepal, is not landlocked. —Rachel Strutt

## Pão de Açúcar Market & Brazilian Buffet

57 Union Square | 617.625.0022
Hours: Mon-Sat, 7am-10pm; Sun, 8am-5pm
Owner/from: Francisco Silva, Brazil
Most customers hail from: Brazil, yet Francisco makes a point of saying all are welcome!
What you'll find: Cured meats for feijoada, various forms of açai (superfruit from Brazil's rain forests), perfume and soccer shirts.
Don't miss: Pão de queijo and coxinha (chicken dumplings)

In addition to fresh pão de queijo—addictive cheese puffs made with yucca flour rather than wheat flour— this market also sells a frozen variety as well as a mix for making your own. Shoppers will also find kits to make feijoada, the undisputed national dish of Brazil. Originating from Bahia, in eastern Brazil, it's made with various pork products (sometimes beef products too) and black beans. The market sells prepared feijoada at its buffet every Saturday; on the side, be sure to have some farofa (which has a consistency similar to farina cereal and is made from manioc/cassava flour). There is an extensive selection of herbs imported from Brazil. Also consider sampling Guarana, Brazil's popular, highly caffeinated soda. —Sharon Wolfson

## Reliable Market

45 Union Square | 617.623.9620
Hours: Mon-Fri, 9.30am-9pm; Sat, 9am-9pm; Sun, 10am-7pm
Owner/from: Young Sook Park, Korea
Most customers hail from: Korea, Japan, China, and Somerville
What you'll find: Bulgoki (thinly sliced beef or pork marinated in salty/sweet sauce), prepared kimchee pancakes, seaweed laver for sushi, frozen gyoza
Don't miss: A staggering selection of sake, rice, noodles and kimchi—and pocky sticks!

Shopping at the Reliable Market is like a vicarious trip to Asia. The shelves are laden with exotic products with labels in a variety of languages. The produce is inexpensive and fresh. Asian staples such as daikon radish, scallions, ginger, tofu and Asian pears are always on hand. Aisle two has rice toppings galore including bonito (salty fish) flakes, wasabi and rice crackers. Reliable also has an entire aisle dedicated to kimchi, a mind-boggling array of noodles and rice, sashimi-grade fish, an excellent selection of Pocky and Pepero cookie sticks (hailing from Japan and Korea, respectively) and elegant and utilitarian crockery. —Rachel Strutt

Left: a towering stack of rice bags at Reliable Market; right: an aisle at Pão de Açúcar.

## Ricky's Flower Market

238 Washington St. | 617.628.7569 | www.rickysflowermarket.com
Hours: **Daily, 7am-7pm**
Owner/from: **Ricky DiGiovanni, Somerville**
What you'll find: **Over 30 different types of tomato plants, along with other vegetables and herbs**

Not everyone sees an out-of-business gas station and thinks, "That would make a great nursery!" But that's precisely what Ricky DiGiovanni did when driving through Union Square one day back in 1990. DiGiovanni bought the old gas station and pursued his idea. Now, a few decades and lot of sweat equity later, he oversees a bustling nursery selling flowers, vegetables and herbs. All the plants are grown in Massachusetts, and choices include honeydew melon, white eggplant and a broad spectrum of tomatoes, from Early Girl to Black Krim. The herb selection is also huge and includes orange mint, lemon mint, sorrel and spicy globe (Greek) basil. DiGiovanni says he often stocks items on request; a recent example is Portuguese kale.
—*Rachel Strutt*

## Sherman Market

22 Union Square | 617.776.4944
Hours: **Mon-Fri, 10am-8pm; Sat, 10am-6pm; Sun, 12pm-6pm.**
Owners/from: **Karyn Coughlin (Massachusetts) and Ben Dryer (Wisconsin)**
Most customers hail from: **Union Square**
What you'll find: **Local and fresh produce, cheese, milk and meats**
Don't miss: **Lavender Honey and Chili Burrata—mozzarella stuffed with mascarpone, lavendar-infused honey and hot chili flakes, made by Somerville's Fiorre di Nonno**

The ultimate locavore market, Sherman specializes in locally grown and produced goods. Their meat selection is especially strong and includes local ground beef, pork and whole chickens—as well as harder-to-get items like rabbit, quail, tongue and chicken hearts. The market also features a wide variety of store-made products like cream cheeses, English muffins, pickles, hummus and various stocks for soups. Produce is seasonal, and items on the shelves change accordingly. If you cannot find what you want, the staff is happy to special order for you—as long as it's local! —*Elysian McNiff*

## Swirl and Slice: A Union Square Specialty Food Market

Union Square Plaza | 617.955.0080 | www.unionsquaremain.org/food/farmers-market
Hours: **Thu, 5pm-8pm; June through September**
Organizers: **Union Square Main Streets and the City of Somerville**
Most customers hail from: **Somerville**
What you'll find: **Organic and local vegetables, fruits, meats and cheeses, all cultivated and produced in Massachusetts**
Don't miss: **Local snacks, baked goods and locally grown cut flowers**

Swirl & Slice offers locally produced foods like breads, baked goods, cheeses, wines, honey and preserves—items that sometimes don't get the limelight they deserve at regular farmers' markets. But this market is not only a place to stock up for your next picnic—Swirl and Slice is an evening out that features live music, tastings, workshops and educational programs, including the Somerville Arts Council's International Market Tours. —*Raleigh Strott*

## Taza Chocolate

561 Windsor St. | 617.284.2232 | www.tazachocolate.com
Hours: Wed-Fri, 11am-6pm, Sat-Sun, 10am-6pm
Owners/from: Alex Whitmore (Boston), Larry Slotnick (New York City), and Kathleen Fulton (South Shore)
Most customers hail from: Taza chocolate is sold nationwide
What you'll find: Organic, stone-ground Mexican chocolate
Don't miss: Salt and Pepper Chocolate Mexicano

A bean-to-bar chocolate manufacturer, Taza is an eco-friendly, community-centric business that uses a traditional Mexican stone grinding technique to produce rich, intense chocolate. Committed to fair trade, Taza imports its beans directly from growers in the Dominican Republic and its sugar from Green Cane Project, a Brazilian organic company. Taza's Mexicano chocolate comes in wide variety of flavors, from the sweet-salty smoothness of a Salted Almond to the smoky-fruity heat of Chipotle Chili. Don't miss their plain dark chocolate either— ranging from 60% to 87% cocoa content, the bars have a powerful and complex taste that combines wonderfully with the rustic, grainy texture that is the trademark of all Taza chocolate. Their periodic chocolate factory tours are not to be missed!
—Sarah Champion

## Union Square Farmers' Market

Union Square Plaza | 617.955.0080 | www.unionsquaremain. org/food/farmers-market
Hours: Sat, 9am-1pm; June through November
Organizers: Union Square Main Streets and the City of Somerville
Most customers hail from: Somerville
What you'll find: Organic and local vegetables, fruits, meats and cheeses, all cultivated and produced in Massachusetts
Don't miss: The new products and vendors at the market this year, including cheeses from Robinson Farm, meats from Hollis Hills Farm and Misty Brook Farm and raw uncut oysters from Shady Oaks Farm, not to mention Culinary Cruisers—mobile, bike-powered snack carts

The Union Square Farmers' Market transforms what was once a sleepy weekend morning to a weekly block party! Each weekend, approximately 2,000 people visit the square in search of Massachusetts-produced goods ranging from baby bok choy and misuna to fresh mozzarella and raw oysters. "Our farmers tell us that this is their most profitable farmers' market," says Mimi Graney, executive director of Union Square Main Streets. "The farmers also tell us that the people who come to this market really know their food." —Raleigh Strott

## WellFoods Plus (Halal Market)

380 Somerville Ave. | 617.666.7700
Hours: Mon-Fri, 10am-9pm; Sat-Sun, 9am-9pm
Owners/from: Rokeya and Jahangir Kabir, Bangladesh
Most customers hail from: Bangladesh, Pakistan, Nepal, India and the Middle East
What you'll find: Halal meat (which undergoes a special butchering process according to Islamic law), goat, fish, tahini, couscous, spices, rice, teas and sweets
Don't miss: The broad assortment of spices and the giant lakka fish in the freezer section

On average, Rokeya and Jahingir Kabir sell three whole goats, or 100 pounds, per day! This is where many local Bengalis, Pakistanis, Haitians and Nepalese buy goat meat. In the back of the store, freezers are stocked with 60 different fish, shipped from Bangladesh and Thailand. Ask them to pull out the four-foot -long, 30-pound fish called lakka, which requires many hours to cook. Bangladesh is predominantly Muslim, so the food at Halal Market varies quite a bit from Indian markets. For instance, Muslims eat beef, whereas Hindus do not. Hence, you'll find beef here, along with Middle Eastern items, including rose water and tahini. —Sharon Wolfson & Rachel Strutt

Taza Chocolate founders Larry Slotnick (left) and Alex Whitmore.

In addition to these markets, don't forget to visit Jerry's Liquor Store—where you'll find ingredients to make the cocktails featured in this book—and the wondrous Market Basket.

## Jerry's Liquor Store

329 Somerville Ave. | 617.666.5410
Hours: Mon-Wed, 9am-10pm, Thu-Sat, 9am-11pm, Sun, 12-6pm

## Market Basket

400 Somerville Ave. | 617.666.2420
Hours: Mon-Sat, 7am-9pm; Sun, 7am-7pm

# Restaurants

Shape Up Somerville is the city's campaign to encourage healthy eating and living. Part of this initiative is the Shape Up Approved campaign, which helps make Somerville a healthy place to live, work, play and eat by tagging healthy menu options at participating restaurants. Shape Up Approved dishes incorporate lean protein, whole grains, fruits and vegetables and low-fat dairy. Please note the Shape Up Approved selections in this guide—and look for the Shape Up decal in Somerville restaurant windows and on menus throughout town.

## The Bearded Pig

445 Somerville Ave. | 617.996.9080 | www.thebeardedpig.com
Hours: Sun-Wed, 11am-9pm; Thu-Sat, 11am-10pm
Owner/from: Michael Schmidt, Jacksonville, Florida
Recommended dish: Pulled Pork or Brisket Sandwich; Banana Pudding for dessert
Shape Up Somerville selections: Pulled Chicken, North Carolina Vinegar Slaw, Collard Greens

The Bearded Pig is a counter-service restaurant that grew out of owner Michael Schmidt's catering business of the same name. Schmidt learned to cook barbecue while growing up in a restaurant family in Jacksonville, Florida. He became an architect and lived and worked in New England for three years before deciding to open The Bearded Pig Catering Company in Kitchen Inc., a shared kitchen facility in Union Square. After seven months as a strictly catering business, Schmidt decided it was time to open a restaurant. The Bearded Pig restaurant serves a condensed version of the catering menu, featuring barbecue classics like pulled pork, pulled chicken, brisket, ribs and traditional sides. For those with room left, desserts include cornbread and banana pudding. —*Shannon Cain Arnold*

## Bloc 11 Café

11 Bow St. | 617.623.0000 | www.bloc11.com
Hours: Fri-Wed, 7am–8 pm; Thu, 7am-9pm
Owners/from: Tucker Lewis (Cambridge) and Jennifer Park (Arlington)
Recommended dish: Poplar salad
Reccomended drink: Espresso Con Panna—a double shot of espresso topped with whipped cream
Shape Up Somerville selection: The Willow—curry tofu salad on whole wheat bread with avocado, apple, sprouts and greens

It was love at first sight when owners Tucker Lewis and Jennifer Park visited a former bank building on Bow Street and saw the potential for a lively, community-oriented café. Now a bustling eco-friendly establishment, Bloc 11 serves a variety of coffee, beverages plus many teas such as Rooibos Flowers and White Peony. In addition to breakfast items like oatmeal, pastries and seasonal fruit parfaits, Bloc 11 has a creative selection of soups and salads. The café also features an extensive sandwich menu including the Clover, a baguette with mozzarella, sundried tomato pesto, tomato, greens and caramelized onions. You can enjoy your meal in the old bank vault, now a cozy dining area, or outside on the comfortable patio. —*Sarah Champion*

Left: Jerry's Liquor Store is draped with grape vines each summer and fall; above: the morning rush at Bloc 11 Café, located in an old bank building.

## Buk Kyung Korean Restaurant

9A Union Square | 617.623.7220 | www.bukkyungrestaurant.com
Hours: Mon, Wed-Sat, 11:30am-10:30pm; Sun, 11:30am-9:45pm; closed Tuesdays
Owner/from: Kyung Suk Lee, Seoul, South Korea
Recommended dish: Jambong—spicy noodle soup with squid, shrimp, mussels and vegetables
✿ Shape Up Somerville selection: Seafood Dolsot Bibimbop—baby shrimp, mussels and squid with sautéed vegetables, red beans and rice served in a sizzling hot stone bowl

Opened by Kyung Suk Lee and her husband in 1998, Buk Kyung offers a menu of over 70 Korean dishes. Traditional menu items include Bulgogi, a savory dish of marinated beef stir-fried with mushrooms, onions and scallions served with rice, and Kimchi, a spicy pickled cabbage dish that accompanies most entrees. Specialties popular from South Korea include Jajangmyun, a Chinese-influenced dish of rice noodles with pork, onion, potatoes and zucchini in a sweet black bean sauce. Many items are served family style, and scissors are included as a utensil for taming the long noodles served with many meals. —Raleigh Strott

## Bull McCabe's Pub

366A Somerville Ave. | 617.440.6045 | www.bullmccabesboston.com
Hours: Mon-Fri, 3pm-1am; Sat-Sun, 11am-1am
Owners/from: Brian Manning and family, Arlington
Recommended dish: House-marinated steak tips
Recommended drink: Chimay Bleue—a classic Belgian brew
✿ Shape Up Somerville selection: Homemade Veggie Burger—made fresh with garbanzo beans, lentils, peppers and onions and seasoned with Tex-Mex spices, on whole wheat bread

A family-owned pub open since 2008, Bull McCabe's produces homemade food and offers an extensive beer list. Burgers are served with a choice of six cheeses and a wide range of toppings. The menu also goes beyond traditional pub fare, with entrees like Filet Mignon. Owner Brian Manning, an area native of Irish heritage, likes pairing great food with great beer. With space at a premium, the options on tap are limited to 10, but Manning stocks 60 varieties of bottled beer. Bull McCabe's also offers local music galore. The pub is known for evenings such as Dub Apocalypse on Sundays and Dub Down on Thursdays and frequently features popular local bands. Bull McCabe's also hosts Stump! Trivia on Monday nights. —Sarah Champion

## Café Tango

16 Bow St.| 781.605.8062
Hours: Daily, 9am–midnight
Owner/from: Vicky Magaletta, Argentina
Recommended dish: Crepes with Nutella and Argentinian dulce de leche; paninis and wraps
Recommended drink: Café con Leche Argentino—similar to café latte, with Argentine coffee; Yerba Mate tea

Vicky Magaletta has brought music and rhythm to Union Square for several years, running the Dance Union Studio and the Tango Society of Boston on Bow Street. In 2012, she expanded her repertoire to include Café Tango, a coffee shop serving a variety of coffees, teas, crepes, sandwiches and desserts. Magaletta opened the café downstairs from her dance studio for a number of reasons, the most important being "to have a place that is a bit different from other cafés, with the purpose of exposing the customers to different cultures." The space, decorated with items Magaletta has collected in her travels, has a distinctive dance and music theme. Café Tango offers live music, lectures and other cultural activities and is open until midnight for those looking for a late-night coffee or dessert. —Shannon Cain Arnold

## Cantina La Mexicana

247 Washington St. | 617.776.5232 | www.cantinalamexicana.com
Hours: Daily, 11am–midnight
Owners/from: Roberto Rendón (Brownsville, Texas) and Carolina Rendón (Mexico)
Recommended dish: Camarónes y Nopales—shrimp and cactus in a chile ancho sauce over rice
Recommended drink: Fig Margarita
✿ Shape Up Somerville selection: Parilla Combo—grilled mixed vegetables with grilled chicken and corn tortillas

Owners Roberto and Carolina Rendón opened Cantina La Mexicana as a counter-service taqueria over a decade ago and recently transformed it into a sit-down restaurant with a colorful interior and an extensive food and cocktail menu. The lineup includes longstanding favorites like the Burro, a burrito of epic proportions; tacos filled with rice, beans and your choice of meat; and Enchiladas Potosinas, prepared in the style of Carolina Rendón's home state, San Luis Potosí, Mexico. Cantina La Mexicana houses a bar adorned with a wide variety of tequilas and serves nearly a dozen different margaritas, including spicy jalapeño. Cantina La Mexicana also features live music on Thursday, Friday and Saturday nights. —Raleigh Strott

Francisco de la Barra

Heather Balchunas

Rachel Strutt

From left to right: Buk Kyung Korean Restaurant; a small crowd outside Bull McCabe's; a Masala Dosa at Dosa Temple waiting to be devoured.

## Casa B

253 Washington St. | 617.623.9710 | www.casabrestaurant.com
Hours: Sun, Tue-Wed, 6pm-10pm; Thu-Sat, 6pm-11pm; late night Fri and Sat, 11pm-1am; closed Mondays
Owner/from: Alberto Cabré (San Juan, Puerto Rico) and Angelina Jockovich (Barranquilla, Colombia)
Recommended dish: Camarón Relleno de Yuca—yucca-stuffed shrimp wrapped in bacon, served with cilantro ginger dipping sauce
Recommended drink: Cilantro-Jalapeño Martini
🍴 Shape Up Somerville selection: Pollo a la Parrilla con Salsa de Aceitunas—grilled chicken with rustic green olive tapenade

Owned by the husband-and-wife team of Angelina Jockovich and Alberto Cabré, Casa B showcases the couple's cultural backgrounds and their training in architecture. Casa B has two floors: a cozy space on the first floor, and a more formal dining room downstairs that features a "living wall" of plants. The restaurant serves small plates that represent Latin American and Caribbean cuisines, including Carne Mechada, a Puerto Rican pot roast stuffed with porcini mushrooms and topped with yucca gnocchi and a red wine sauce, and the Sandwich de Bistec, with crispy shallots and beef tenderloin. —Rebecca Small

## Dosa Temple

447 Somerville Ave. | 617.764.3152 | www.dosatemple.com
Hours: Mon-Thu, 11:30am-3pm and 5pm-10pm; Fri-Sun, 11:30am-10:30pm; delivery: Mon-Fri, 5pm-10pm; Sat-Sun, 12pm-10pm
Owner/from: Gopal Krishnan, Tamilnadu, India
Recommended dishes: Sundal—chickpeas, roasted onion, coconut and spices; dosas—fermented crepes with various fillings
Recommended drinks: Mango Lassi; Chickoo Shake—Fresh milk and chickoo fruit
🍴 Shape Up Somerville selection: Baingan Bhartha—minced eggplant in a tomato sauce with green peas, served with chapati

Dosa Temple first opened in the central Massachusetts town of Ashland in 2007. Owner Gopal Krishnan opened a second location in Union Square in 2012. The restaurant features vegetarian and vegan South Indian cuisine, including sundal and dosas. Dosa Temple also offers other Indian favorites such as Mutter Paneer, peas and Indian cheese in an onion and tomato sauce; and Malai Kofta, vegetable balls and cheese in an almond sauce, as well as rice specialties and Indian desserts. A lunch buffet, available Friday through Sunday for $12 per person, comes with fresh dosas.
—Shannon Cain Arnold

## Ebi Sushi

290 Somerville Ave. | 617.764.5556 | www.ebisushi.com
Hours: Daily lunch 11:30am-3:30pm; dinner 5pm-10pm; delivery Mon-Fri, 5pm-10pm; Sat-Sun, 12pm-10pm
Owner/from: José García, Puerto Barrios, Guatemala
Recommended dish: Agedashi Tofu—tofu served in broth and topped with bonito flakes; Okonomiyaki—pancake made from cabbage and pork with Japanese sauce and bonito flakes
Shape Up Somerville selection: Big Yakitori—grilled skewers of chicken with scallions; served with rice and salad

Ebi Sushi owner Jose Garcia moved to the United States from Guatemala in 2000 and has been in the sushi business ever since. Located in a simple, elegant space on Somerville Avenue, Ebi features an extensive sushi menu, including the Spider Roll, with softshell crab and cucumber, and a vegetable roll with sweet potato tempura, cucumber, avocado, eel sauce and spicy mayo. Ebi also serves a variety of main dishes ranging from Sashimi Squid to Mackerel Fillet to Ginger Pork. These entrées are complemented by small plates including tempura, noodle soups and curry rice dishes, which are an adaptation of the Indian favorite and considered a national dish in Japan. Ebi Sushi also offers delivery. —*Elysian McNiff*

## El Potro Mexican Grill Restaurant

61 Union Square | 617.666.4200 | www.elpotrosomerville.com
Hours: Daily, 10am-1am
Owner/from: Elias Interiano, El Salvador
Recommended dish: Enchiladas al Mole with Loroco Pupusas
Recommended drink: Horchata—a rice and cinnamon drink
Shape Up Somerville selection: Grilled Chicken Dinner—served with steamed rice, vegetables, salad and corn tortillas

At El Potro you will find vibrant walls adorned with sombreros and portraits of Mexican movie stars, hand-painted chairs from Guadelajara and, if you're there on a weekend, live mariachi music by Mariachi Estampa de America. Don't miss Salvadoran items like pupusas—tortillas stuffed with cheese and either beans or loroco, a plant whose flowers are used extensively in Salvadoran cuisine. Tex-Mex dishes are available as well: nachos, quesadillas, enchiladas, fajitas, tacos and burritos, plus desserts like flan and fried ice cream. El Potro also offers full bar service. The restaurant is open for breakfast too, offering items such as Desayuno Ranchero, eggs scrambled with tomatoes and onions, served with a slice of plantain. —*Jarrett Lerner*

Above: a double espresso at Fortissimo Cafe; right: India Palace manager Lal Bahadur Ayer at the lunch buffet.

## Fiesta Bakery

316 Somerville Ave. | 617.623.7800
Hours: Mon-Sat, 8am-9pm; closed Sundays
Owner/from: William Pamphile, Haiti
Recommended dish: Haitian meat patties—delicately spiced, savory meat filling in flaky golden pastry, served with hearty Haitian rice and beans
Recommended drink: Akasan—corn juice, milk and sugar, a cross between a milkshake and pudding

Fiesta Bakery and Restaurant occupies a deceptively small storefront considering the wide array of foods available inside. In addition to the Akasan, cookies and meat patties on display, Fiesta specializes in all manner of decorated cakes made to order for special occasions. Owner William Pamphile also runs a thriving catering business that serves traditional Haitian fare such as Riz au Djon djon, rice with djon djon mushrooms; Calalou, beef stew with mushrooms; and Tassot Gabrit, fried goat. Pamphile also runs Vision Youth Builders of Haiti, a nongovernmental organization that provides a variety of education, health and social service programs for youth and families in Port-au-Prince, Haiti. —*Rebecca Small*

## Fortissimo Café

365 Somerville Ave.| 617.776.1880 | www.facebook.com/fortissimocoffeehouse
Hours: Mon-Fri, 7am-7pm; Sat, 7am-4pm; closed Sundays
Owner/from: Vinny Soares, Brazil
Recommended dishes: Pão de Queijo
Recommended drink: Anything with espresso
Shape Up Somerville selections: Green Street Sandwich — arugula, spinach, tomato, onions, cucumber, and peppers in a whole wheat wrap; Guava spread (raisins and apricots)

Vinny Soares opened Fortissimo in April 2012 in the space previously occupied by his parents' Brazilian bakery. Soares has kept many Brazilian baked goods on the menu, including corn cakes and Pão de Queijo (Brazilian cheese bread), though he lets baker Toni Duarte use his creativity to come up with different items daily. This coffee shop also has a substantial sandwich menu including the Uncle Toni, a panini with chipotle turkey, chipotle gouda, onion, tomato, romaine, red and yellow peppers and guava cream cheese. Soares, a drummer, brings music into the café in more than just its name—he keeps a working record player in one corner and encourages customers to bring and play their own records. —*Shannon Cain Arnold*

## The Independent

75 Union Square | 617.440.6022 | www.theindo.com
Hours: Mon-Thu, 3pm-1am; Fri, 3pm-2am; Sat, 11am-2am; Sun, 11am-1am
Owner/from: Ken Kelly, Ireland
Recommended dish: Daily seafood special, steak frites
Recommended drink: The Union—a drink created by cocktail historian Brother Cleve to reflect the Square's immigrants
Shape Up Somerville selection: Quinoa Salad—quinoa, shaved fennel, grapefruit and mint walnut citrus vinaigrette

One side is a cozy wood-paneled bar; the other a spacious restaurant. The menu includes appetizers like mussels cooked in a variety of styles, and bacon-sprinkled deviled eggs. Entrees change seasonally but you can always find a burger made from grass-fed beef from Hanson and Roberts Farm, chicken from Seven Acre Farms and a daily special of locally caught, sustainable seafood. The bar boasts 32 draft beers and over 60 bottles, with most on a seasonal rotation alongside Belgian classics such as Duvel and local favorites like Pretty Things. The bar also serves creative cocktails and organically produced wines from sustainable vineyards. —*Sarah Champion*

## India Palace

23 Union Square | 617.666.9770 | www.indiapalaceinsomerville.com
Hours: Mon-Sat, 11am-3pm, 5pm-11pm; Sun,12pm-11pm ; free delivery 5pm-11pm
Owner/from: Gurdev Singh, India
Recommended dish: Chicken Tikka Masala—diced white-meat chicken cooked in a creamy sauce with tomato and coriander
Recommended drink: Mango Lassi
Shape Up Somerville selection: Shrimp Jalfrezi—jumbo shrimp cooked with fresh vegetables and exotic Indian spices

India Palace offers a wide variety of dishes from Northern India, including Chicken Tikka Masala, succulent chicken cooked in a rich, creamy sauce with tomato and coriander, and Chicken Korma, cooked with nuts, raisins and a mix of herbs and spices in a creamy sauce. There are also many vegetarian options, including Palak Paneer, fresh spinach with homemade cheese and coriander. India Palace also serves freshly baked breads, tandoori specialties, rice dishes and tempting desserts. All dishes can be cooked to your preferred level of spiciness. India Palace also offers a daily all-you-can-eat lunch buffet featuring a selection of appetizers, entrees and desserts for $7.95. —*Valeria Amato*

## Jimbo's Famous Roast Beef & Seafood

40 Bow St. | 617.623.9068 | www.jimbosroastbeefsomerville.com
Hours: Mon-Thu,11am-9:30pm; Sat, 11am-10:30pm; Sun, 12pm-8:30pm
Owner/from: Harkirit Singh, India
Recommended dish: Roast beef
☻ Shape Up Somerville selection: Kabob salad with chicken or shrimp, light Italian and other dressing on the side with a wheat wrap

Jimbo's is mainly a takeout and delivery spot serving roast beef, pizza, seafood, wings and subs. Customers can choose from a variety of creative pizzas including the Mexican with olives, tomatoes, onions, jalapeños and taco meat, and the Spinach Alfredo pizza with alfredo sauce, mozzarella cheese, bacon, mushrooms and spinach. The various seafood options include a Captain's Platter with haddock, shrimp, scallops and Ipswich clams, served with fries, onion rings and coleslaw. Staff and customers recommend you try one of Jimbo's roast beef sandwiches, available with a variety of toppings.
—*Shannon Cain Arnold*

## Journeyman/backbar

9 Sanborn Ct. | 617.718.2333 | www.journeymanrestaurant.com
Hours: Wed-Mon, 5:30pm-10pm; backbar open Wed-Mon 4pm-midnight; closed Tuesdays
Owners/From: Diana Kudajarova (Riga, Latvia), Tse Wei Lim (Singapore) and Meg Grady-Troia (New York City)
Recommended dish at Journeyman: Seasonal selections
Recommended drink at backbar: Tequila Mockingbird
☻ Shape Up Somerville selection: Spring Salad

Journeyman occupies a spare, elegant space hidden in a small alley off Union Square. Celebrating local, seasonal foods, it offers a frequently changing tasting menu; diners choose a three-, five- or seven-course menu, either omnivore or vegetarian. Past menu highlights include pumpkin and squash soup served with fried oysters and brown butter and foie gras served with a warm veal broth. In 2011, Journeyman's owners expanded their space to include backbar, a craft cocktail bar that features creative libations like the Scofflaw—Old Overholt rye, lemon, dry vermouth and pomegranate—and small plates and charcuterie from Journeyman. You'll also find savvy mixologists like Sam Treadway and a gorgeous chalkboard menu, thanks to local artist Catherine Owens. —*Jarrett Lerner*

## Machu Picchu Charcoal Chicken & Grill

25 Union Square | 617.623.7972 | www.machuchicken.com
Hours: Sun-Fri, 12:pm-10pm; Sat, 12pm-11pm
Owner/from: Rosy Cerna, Lima, Peru
Recommended dish: Pollo a la Brasa—chicken grilled on charcoal
Recommended drink: Chicha Morada—a sweet refreshing drink made with purple corn
☻ Shape Up Somerville selection: Chicken Misky—a quarter chicken (dark or white) accompanied with a salad

Machu Picchu owner Rosy Cerna says restaurants that serve only chicken, called *pollerias*, are common in Peru. This Union Square *polleria* marinates its chicken in a mix that includes Peruvian beer and rosemary for up to 24 hours and serves it with a choice of two insanely good sauces—a green one made with jalapeño and the Andean herb huacatay, and a yellow huancaína sauce flavored with Peru's most famous chili: ají amarillo. This restaurant also serves Andean Chicken Salad made with Peruvian quinoa and Anticuchos Peruanos, beef hearts that come sliced and on skewers. For dessert, try the Peruvian Flan, which is a little browner than traditional flan and sits in a pool of caramelized sugar.
—*Rachel Strutt*

## Machu Picchu Restaurante Turistico

307 Somerville Ave. | 617.628.7070 | www.machupicchuboston.com
Hours: Sun-Thu, 11:30am-10pm; Fri-Sat, 11:30am-midnight
Owner/from: Rosy Cerna, Lima, Peru
Recommended dish: Ceviche—raw fish marinated in lime juice and served with sweet potato, toasted corn and rocoto pepper
Recommended drink: Pisco Sour
☻ Shape Up Somerville selection: Quinua Andina—a versatile, nutritious and tasty grain from Peru known as the gold of the Incas, this stew is made with chicken

At Machu Picchu, owner Rosy Cerna shares the distinctive flavors and rich culinary heritage of her native Peru. On Friday nights you can hear a traditional Andean band while sipping on a pisco sour and enjoying the Peruvian national dish, ceviche. Ever since moving to Somerville from Lima, Cerna has been creating traditional dishes that span the three different regions of her native country: coast, mountains and jungle. Taste Peruvian corn served with queso fresco, a classic food of the Andes; or Causa Limeña, a famous coastal dish whose name means "sustenance of life" in Spanish. Or nibble on some fried yucca, a jungle favorite. —*Elysian McNiff*

Left: Sam Treadway, a backbar bartender and winner of the 2012 Great Improper Bartending Competition; below: the Andean Chicken Salad at Machu Picchu Chicken and Grill.

## Neighborhood Restaurant and Bakery

25 Bow St. | 617.623.9710 | www.theneighborhoodrestaurant.com
Hours: Daily, 7am-4pm
Owner/from: Sheila Borges Foley, Newark, New Jersey (Her father is from the Azores)
Recommended dish: Portuguese Cream of Wheat
Recommended drink: Homemade wine
Shape Up Somerville selections: Multigrain Oatmeal Waffle with fresh fruit; Scrambled Egg Whites with tomatoes, spinach, cheese and a side of turkey bacon

The Neighborhood Restaurant and Bakery originally opened its doors as a storefront selling baked treats in 1983. The Neighborhood's unique family recipes include homemade jelly, syrups, Portuguese sweet breads, wines, soups and sauces. At breakfast, make sure to order the Papage, a Portuguese cereal similar to Cream of Wheat made with a closely guarded family recipe. For lunch, treat yourself to one of the homemade soups. In the later hours of the day, you can sit in the shade of the patio and drink homemade wine made from the grapes hanging over your head while enjoying one of Sheila Borges Foley's seafood or linguica plates. —Elysian McNiff

## Precinct

70 Union Square | 617.623.9211 | www.precinctbar.com
Hours: Mon-Thu, 4pm-1am; Fri, 3pm-2am; Sat, 11am-2am; Sun, 11am-1am
Owner/from: Ken Kelly, Ireland
Recommended dish: Spinach and Artichoke Dip
Recommended drink: Local New England beers and classic cocktails from the '70s and '80s with a twist
Shape Up Somerville selection: Grilled Salmon with Lentils, Fennel & Citrus Salad

Precinct, located in a former police station and jailhouse, offers an outdoor patio great for people-watching; two bars serving creative cocktails and over 60 varieties of beer; a live music venue featuring local bands daily; delicious food (dinner, brunch and late-night) focusing on local products and homemade preparations; and televisions galore to watch your favorite sporting events. Appetizers include Spinach and Artichoke Dip and a Kobe Beef Hot Dog on a griddled bun. For a main course, entrees range from Seared Scallops to Pork Schnitzel with arugula, pickled onions and caper aioli. Precinct also serves a weekend brunch featuring several varieties of Bloody Marys and Mimosas. —Elysian McNiff

Left: the patio at Precinct; top: Jimbo's Roast Beef; below: the satisfying Irish burger at Sally O'Briens.

## Sally O'Brien's

335 Somerville Ave. | 617.666.3589 | www.sallyobriensbar.com
Hours: Daily, 11am-1am
Owner/from: Liam Mannion, Galway, Ireland
Recommended dishes: Cajun Shrimp Dinner, burgers
Recommended drink: Bloody Mary
Shape Up Somerville selection: Grilled Shrimp—Buffalo or Cajun style—served over steamed rice with salad

Sally O's is a large restaurant and bar on Somerville Avenue that serves classic Irish, Mexican, Italian and American food. Known for its burgers—eight-ounce patties served on a toasted bun with a variety of toppings to choose from—the restaurant also offers seasonal specials. Shepherd's Pie and Beef Stew are winter favorites; fish specials and salads are popular in the summer. Sally O's is also well known for its live music, which attracts diverse crowds five nights a week. Local bands hit the stage every night except Monday, when the crowd is invited to step up for a comedy open mike, and Wednesday, which is free poker night. —*Véra Vidal*

## Sherman Cafe

257 Washington St. | 617.776.4944 | www.facebook.com/shermancafe
Hours: Mon-Fri, 7am-6pm; Sat-Sun, 8am-6pm
Owners/from: Karyn Coughlin (Massachusetts) and Ben Dryer (Wisconsin)
Recommended dish: Creative sandwiches that change seasonally
Recommended drink: Cantaloupe-Mint Soda
Shape Up Somerville selection: Green Hummus Sandwich—hummus, herbs, spinach, red pepper spread, carrot, cucumber, onion and greens on seven-grain bread

The chalkboard menu on the wall boasts seasonal sandwiches, salads and brunch items all made from local and fresh products. Though the menu changes frequently, past favorites have included the Pressed Gruyere Sandwich and the Maine-based Pineland Farms Swiss Cheese Sandwich. Sherman Cafe can also give you your morning dose of caffeine, like a light roast from Amherst-based Rao's coffee, or midday tea from Somerville-based MEM Tea Imports. Sherman also offers home-baked sweets and treats like English muffins, strawberry scones and vegan mocha cupcakes. —*Elysian McNiff*

## Sweet Ginger

22 Bow St.| 617.625.5015 | www.sweetgingerunionsq.com
Hours: Mon-Thu, 11:30am-9:30pm; Fri, 11:30am-10pm; Sat, 12pm-10pm; Sun, 4:30pm-9pm
Owner/from Rungnapa Otero and Patchara Thavornkas, Thailand
Recommended dishes: Pad Thai, Tamarind duck
Recommended drink: Thai Iced Tea—a black tea drink sweetened with sugar and condensed milk
Shape Up Somerville selection: Seafood Volcano—sauteed shrimp, mussels, squid and scallops with baby corn, snow peas, mushroom, carrot, onion, bell peppers and basil in spicy sauce

This restaurant makes good on its name, blending sweet and spicy foods. Take the popular Crab Rangoon, for example, made with crabmeat and cream cheese wrapped in a wonton skin, gets a twist with added curry powder and onion to give the dish more bite. Heat seekers will enjoy fiery dishes like the Drunken Chicken sautéed with vegetables in a Thai chili paste or the Pad Kra-Pow, a Thai-style stir-fry with peppers in a spicy sauce. The menu also features a wide selection of seafood, including the Tilapia Fillet with Mango Salsa and Spicy Squid served with vegetables and a Thai chili sauce. —Elysian McNiff

Seaweed rolls with ginger sauce at Sweet Ginger.

## Coming Soon

Bronwyn, the newest restaurant from the folks who run TWFood in Cambridge, will feature food grounded in the local community with elements of German and Eastern European cuisine, a full bar and patio, as well as a traditional dining room and a wine list including lesser-known varietals from Eastern Europe. Part of the menu will be dedicated to handmade fresh sausages like Thruinger and Weisswurst. There will also be vegetarian options, like whole-grain risotto with pumpkin.

## In addition to the venues profiled here, you can find the following restaurants in the Square:

### Buddy's Truck Stop
112 Washington St. | 617.623.9725
Hours: Mon-Sat, 5am-2pm; Sun, 7am-2pm

### Ceasar's Pizza
401 Somerville Ave. | 617.776.9942
Hours: Mon-Sat, 10am-9pm; Sun, 11am-5pm

### Dunkin Donuts
282 Somerville Ave. | 617.623.9703 | www.dunkindonuts.com
Hours : 24/7

### J & J Restaurant
157 Washington St. | 617.625.3978 | www.jandjrestaurant.com/
Hours : Mon-Fri, 10am-9pm; Sat-Sun, 9am-9pm

### Mama Gina's Pizza
19 Union Square | 617.625.0116 |
www.mamaginaspizzasomerville.com
Hours: Mon-Sat, 10:30am-10pm; Sun, 12pm-8pm

### Mandarin Chinese Restaurant
7 Union Square | 617.776.8680
Hours: Mon-Thu, 11am-11pm; Fri-Sat 11am-12am; Sun, 12pm-11pm

### Pizza Palace
222 Somerville Ave. | 617.628.6464
Hours: Mon-Sat, 11am-10pm; closed Sundays

### Red House Chinese Restaurant
24 Union Square | 617.666.4300
Hours: Mon-Fri, 11am-1:30am; Sat-Sun, 11am-2am

### Subway Sub Shop
71 Union Square | 617.623.1144 | www.subway.com
Hours: Mon-Fri, 7am-10pm; Sat-Sun, 8am-10pm

### Union Square Pizza & Subs
63 Union Square | 617.666.8686 |
www.unionsquare-pizza.com
Hours: Daily, 11am-11pm

# THE SOMERVILLE ARTS COUNCIL

Gregory Jenkins, Executive Director
Rachel Strutt, Program Manager
Heather Balchunas, Office Manager
Meagan O'Brien, ArtsUnion Coordinator

**Hungry for more?**
Visit www.somervilleartscouncil.org/nibble. Here you will find more food stories, recipes, art, interviews—plus information on Union Square food events and market tours.

## ABOUT US

The Somerville Arts Council cultivates and celebrates the creative expressions of the Somerville community. Through innovative collaborations and quality programming we work to make the arts an integral part of life reflective of our diverse city. The Council has been cited by the Massachusetts Cultural Council as a statewide leader, and has received the Commonwealth Award, which recognizes excellence in the arts, humanities and sciences. Many of our programs are made possible by the dedication of our board and community volunteers.

## WE ORGANIZE THE FOLLOWING PROGRAMS

**Art in the Garden** | A summer arts and environmental program held outdoors at the Community Growing Center during July and August. It is open to children ages 6 to 12.

**ArtBeat** | Our annual multimedia arts festival in Davis Square highlighting local artists of all kinds and attracting up to 10,000 people the third weekend in July.

**ArtsUnion** | Arts programming and cultural initiatives designed to spur economic development in Union Square. ArtsUnion produces crafts markets, cultural tours and event series and commissions local artists to design and build street furniture and public art.

**Books of Hope** | A creative-writing and teen empowerment program held at the Mystic Activity Center.

**Culture Club** | A monthly program produced and hosted by the Somerville Arts Council, directed and aired by our ArtsUnion partners, Somerville Community Access Television.

**Illuminations Tour** | A December trolley tour showcasing the city's fabulous holiday lights.

**Inside Out Gallery** | A gallery with monthly exhibits in the CVS windows in Davis Square

**Intercambio** A language and culture exchange, run in conjunction with the Somerville Center for Adult Learning Experiences.

**LCC Grants Program** | Our annual grant program, funded by the MCC. Each fall, we provide grants that support artists and arts programming within the community and schools.

**Mystic River Mural Project** | A summer art and environmental program in which teens explore the Mystic River and help to create a large, ongoing mural located on Mystic Avenue near I-93.

**Nibble** | A blog and book exploring food and culture in Union Square.

**Porchfest** | A citywide festival in which musicians and bands perform on Somerville porches each spring.

Left to right: Pillsbury meets paratha at Little India; a "super horchata" mix at La Internacional; "nude" pepero sticks at Reliable Market; also at the Reliable, a sign that makes us smile.

## W W W . S O M E R V I L L E A R T S C O U N C I L . O R G